WESTERHOPE REMEMBERED

Tom Peacock & Ron Handley

Westerhope Village in the early 1900s – West Avenue (known as Clarty Avenue) with Beaumont Terrace on left with Dicky Rowe's Cottage, Arthur's Buildings and Bensons Buildings on right.

Previous page: Westerhope Methodist Chapel Sunday School in the early 1900s – outside the original Chapel. The Rev Wakenshaw is in the centre.

Front cover:
Top photograph: Westerhope's founders in front of the Red Cow Farm, with Joseph Wakinshaw on far left, Robert Hisco far right and Mrs Clark front centre.
Bottom photograph: The Westerhope Wheel at the entrance to the village. A stone plinth with a descriptive plaque is situated on the opposite right side of the road.

Back cover:
Top photograph: Local History Society outing to Thirlestane Castle near Lauder, the Scottish Borders.
Bottom left: The Millennium Clock at the entrance to the Methodist Church.
Bottom right: Westerhope Proggy Mat which is on display at the entrance to the Westerhope Community Centre.

Copyright Tom Peacock & Ron Handley 2010

First published in 2010 by

Summerhill Books
PO Box 1210, Newcastle-upon-Tyne NE99 4AH

www.summerhillbooks.co.uk

Email: summerhillbooks@yahoo.co.uk

ISBN: 978-1-906721-32-9

Printed by CVN Print Ltd, Maxwell Street, South Shields

No part of this publication may be reproduced, stored in a mechanical retrieval system, or transmitted, in any form or by any means, electronic, mechanical, photocopying, recording or otherwise, without prior permission of the authors.

Contents

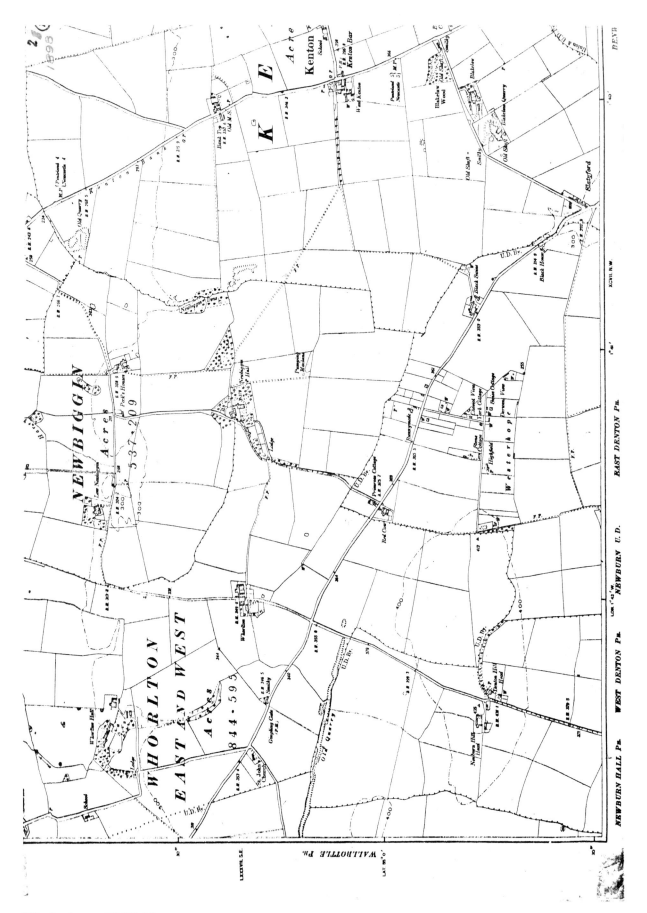

Westerhope 1898 Map.

4

INTRODUCTION

The motivation for producing this history of Westerhope was based on the fact that three ex miner friends, each over 90 years of age, have died in recent years and, with their deaths, a tremendous amount of village history has been lost. To visit Joe Allison, Thomas Jones and Henry Smith was a real privilege. They were a fount of local knowledge and a lot of information within this book was gleaned from visits to their homes. Another person who, fortunately, is still with us (also aged 90) is Desmond Walton. He is not a resident of Westerhope but his grandfather, Robert Hisco, was one of the original founders of the village and built and lived in Kendal Green West which, together with Kendal Green East, are the only three storied dwellings in the village.

Desmond was the Chief Librarian at Denton Park Library and was a founder member of our Local History Society. In that role he collected a large range of photographs of Newcastle West End and, on retirement, helped form the West End Studies Group at Benwell Library. The Group has now been named the West Newcastle Picture History Collection Group and meets at the West End Library on Condercum Road.

An additional incentive to produce this book, was due to the success of the booklet "Westerhope Walkabout", which was produced by the Newcastle Community Heritage Project in conjunction with the Westerhope Community Partnership – 'WCP'.

The majority of the photographs in

Stamfordham Road around 1910 – with Brook's Buildings on right.

the book are from the collection of Ron Handley. Ron is an avid collector of photographs relating to this area, together with historical maps, and also has a host of school photographs dating back to the School on Hillhead Road opening in 1907. He provides a lot of information for many local societies, including the Local History Society of which he is a Committee Member.

It is incredible that such a large selection of photographs has been collected when, in those early days, it was almost unique for anyone to have a camera – at best it would be a 'Box Brownie'. The expense in purchasing a camera and being able to afford the processing and buying the films, would be a deterrent.

Referring to the founders, they would be astonished at the progress that has been made during the past century. They would not have experienced listening to a wireless, as they were not commercially available until the early 1920s. They may not have seen a motor car, as there were only 15 cars on UK roads in 1900.

The transition from those early days to the present is amazing. Gone are their poss tubs and mangles, proggy and clippie mats, press beds, coal fires, the school abacus etc, etc, and what about splitting the atom and space travel. They would have marvelled at the sight of more recent developments – television, computers, mobile phones and home appliances – fridge freezers, automatic washing machines and vacuum cleaners.

With the rate of progress, it would now be impossible to speculate what changes will be made 10 years from now, never mind 100 years.

I am particularly indebted to Councillor Pat Hillicks and Mrs. Sheila Handley for their assistance in typing all of the handwritten notes in difficult circumstances – that of identifying my handwriting! Without their help the production of this book would have been very difficult.

Thanks also to the various Societies for providing notes on their history and to the friends who were prepared to be interviewed to record their and their families history.

I am also grateful for the guidance of Yvonne Young, the author of the books *Benwell Remembered* and *Westenders*.

ACKNOWLEDGEMENTS

Thanks to those who in any way, contributed to the publication of this book.
In particular to:

Dorothy Procter for introducing us to the publisher, Andrew Clark of Summerhill Books.

Len Allison for granting permission to publish his parent's memories.

Westerhope Mature Action Group (MAGS) who organised a history memories morning to help promote the book.

Westerhope Community Partnership (WCP).

West Newcastle Picture History Collection.

Councillor Pat Hillicks and Mrs Sheila Handley for their invaluable assistance in the typing of all the handwritten notes and for their continuing interest in the idea of producing the history of Westerhope Book.

The individual ladies who were prepared to be interviewed to record their and their families history.

Edward Bulloch for the photograph of the Wheel on the front cover and Rev Ann Marr for the photograph of the Proggy Mat on the back cover.

Finally to our respective wives for their understanding for the time spent in researching the material for the book and for the chaos created with the vast collection of photographs and text around our homes for several months.

Thanks to those who contributed in any way to the publication of this book. We apologise for any inaccuracies we may have made in either, the text, captions or photographic dates, which may have occurred due to the passage of time.

An Excelsior trip to Pontin's, Blackpool, around 1954.

WESTERHOPE VILLAGE

Details of the areas history can be traced back to 1765 when its nine farms and several coal mines were owned by a London notability – Mr. Edward Montagu, whose northern home was Denton Hall, until recently occupied by the Roman Catholic Bishop of Newcastle and Hexham. The Hall remained in the Montagu family until the death of Mrs. Montagu in 1800, when it was left to her nephew Matthew Robinson, providing he changed his name to Montagu. He agreed to the change, but eventually became the fourth Lord Rokeby.

However, in 1890, a consulting engineer working in Newcastle and living in Runnymede House on Stamfordham Road, conceived the idea of forming a society to develop smallholdings outside of the city boundary. As a result 'The Northern Allotment Society was founded in 1890 on the 21st May. Their object was, to quote their articles – "to

Stamfordham Road 1905 – 1912 – Boyd Terrace on the right before the Picture Palace 'Orion' was built opposite.

further the growth of fruit and flowers and the cultivation of smallholdings".

In 1891, they purchased 61 acres of land from a Mr. John Tweddle. This land was formerly part of the Montagu estate known as the Red Cow Farm. The 14 members of the NAS came from many areas and as they were not impressed with the name Red Cow Farm, decided to re-name it Westerhope as they considered their new housing and land development to be the 'Hope of the West'. After building several very impressive stone houses, the Society were short of capital, so they decided to auction some of their land – the Red Cow Farm buildings and an area of land at the rear of the farm.

The nearby North Walbottle Colliery had been developed in 1891, and were now looking for land to build houses for their miners and families.

Consequently, they made a successful bid to purchase the land despite the efforts of the NAS to prevent it. They realised that if colliery houses were built on their land it would contrast with the object of creating a garden village.

In 1901, Boyd and Rogerson Terraces were built and the first stage of Beaumont Terrace was commenced.

The building of these terraced houses confirmed the concern of the NAS. Additional terraced houses were built by Mr. Tom Bell – Belmont Cottages, and so the Society abandoned their Westerhope project and moved to develop estates in Darras Hall, Whickham and Rowlands Gill.

It would be interesting to know what Westerhope would have looked like if North Walbottle Colliery Company had not sunk their mines in this area.

Stamfordham Road with Pilton Nurseries, Mr Harris's House, on the left. The date is around 1939-1945. The parade is passing Beaumont Terrace with soldiers marching followed by tanks or bren gun carriers.

PRIMROSE COTTAGE was built in 1860 for the farm hind who worked at the Red Cow Farm, on the opposite side of the road. It still exists at the corner of Stamfordham Road and Newbiggin Lane. This photograph was taken in 1909 and shows Mrs Bella Dickinson with Annie, her niece.

RUNNYMEDE was the first house built for the Northern Allotment Society and its first occupant was Mr Joseph Wakinshaw, the initiator of the Society. It was a prestigious house, stone built, with, as shown, tennis court at its front, extensive gardens and an orchard at the rear. In 1947 it was purchased by Newcastle Breweries, in spite of opposition by local residents. In 1964 it was demolished and replaced by a new Runnymede – a public house. It too was eventually demolished and replaced by an ALDI store.

Above: KENDAL GREEN EAST and WEST are the only three-storey houses in the village. EAST was built for one of the founders – Mrs Clark – and there was a well at its rear, which provided water for the early residents.

WEST was built for another founder, Robert Hisco, who came from Kendal, hence the house name. It is believed that he thought of the name WESTERHOPE as he had come from the WEST with HOPE for the future. A pleasant change from 'The Red Cow Farm Estate'. Robert was the grandfather of Desmond Walton, a local historian.

Right: Mr & Mrs Robert & Statira Hisco around 1896. On the rocking horse is son Ralph and at the front is Peggy (Des Walton's mother).

NORTH WALBOTTLE COLLIERY

The Westerhope area is riddled with ancient shallow bell pits, but the first Walbottle 'deep pit' was working as early as 1760. The old wagonway probably dates from this time, for it is recorded that in 1790 the wooden rails were replaced by the new malleable iron rails. George Stephenson was involved and alongside the wagonway were pits he must have been involved with; Blucher, named after Wellington's colleague in the victory of Waterloo, Coronation, named for the Coronation of William IV and Maria sunk in 1775.

By comparison, North Walbottle was a relatively new modern mine. The first shaft being sunk in 1891 and, at that time, was known as 'The Old Fred Pit', or Jimmy's Pit, named after Jim Bainbridge, the master sinker of the pit shafts. The first coal seam was the Main Coal and in 1892 its output was registered at 2,813 tons. This shaft was

The Colliery was developed from 1891 and closed in August 1968 having produced 21.5 million tons of coal. Its location was in the area now occupied by the St John's Housing Estate Stamfordham Road is in the foreground.

later filled in, but there is no recorded date when that occurred.

The Busty (Betty) pit was opened in 1893 and the Brockwell (Mary) pit was sunk in 1893 and completed in 1894. In 1895 the Beaumont Seam was reached which produced a high quality household coal – so good that in 1909 a gold medal was won, in spite of competition from pits throughout Britain. This seam's financial success also enabled sinking operations in both shafts to reach the Brockwell Seam at a depth of 125 fathoms.

In 1905, the temporary winding engines and pithead were replaced and additions to the heapstead were built later. In the early days, all coal was produced by hand and the putter and pony were indispensable but, in the final days, only 20 ponies existed of the former 150 employed. There was an early attempt at mechanisation in 1905, with a disc machine cutter powered by compressed air, but it was not until 1929 that the pit was fully electrified. In its final days, all coal was machine cut, hand filled and belt conveyed to loading stations.

Owing to highly faulted ground, individual coal faces were generally short lived, few of them producing for more than six months. Five seams were worked ranging from 22 inches to 32 inches high. Some of the seams were three miles distant from the shaft. When the colliery closed in 1968, large coal reserves were still available, mostly in the area of Woolsington, but if these had been exploited, there would have been problems, due to subsidence, for Newcastle Airport.

A putter with pony in limmers attached to a tub.

STATISTICS:

Tonnage from Beaumont Seam in 1895 – 2,496 tons
First coal from Brockwell Seam in 1904 – 3,464 tons 9 cwts
First coal from Bottom Busty Seam in 1912 – 1,221 tons 15 cwts
First coal from Tilly Seam in 1926 – 332 tons 1 cwt
First coal from Top Busty Seam in 1930 – 638 tons 11 cwts
Most coal produced in one year – 413,372 tons 18 cwts
Total tonnage up to March 1967 – 21.5 million tons
Most number of men employed at any time – 1,300
Last day to produce coal – Friday 23rd February 1968

Many social activities could be attributed to the Colliery and, in 1925, the Miners' Welfare Hall was built on Hillhead Road – now the Westerhope Community Centre.

In a newspaper cutting dated 1892, it was stated that "the North Walbottle Coal Company Limited had a share capital of £50,050 in shares of £10 each, which are understood to have been taken up.

"There are about 1,120 acres in the area of the royalty, which belongs to his Grace the Duke of Northumberland. The ground is virgin, no pits having worked there before.

"The railway, which will

Filling shot-fired coal into tubs. Note candle for illumination and no head protection.

extend from the new pit to Lemington and thence to the shipping places on the river, is a portion of the wagon way, which belonged to the Walbottle Coal Company, when the Coronation pit was worked by Messrs. R.O. Lamb and Partners. Messsrs. Robert Fenwick Boyd, Houghton-le-Spring; John Rogerson, Croxdale Hall; William Savile Hargrove, Gosforth; John Edwin Rogerson, Croxdale Hall; and John Swallow, Lintz Green, were the provisional directors.

"The vendors received for their trouble in taking the initial steps, 50 paid-up founders shares of £1 each in all, and they agreed, after the first two years, not to participate in the profits till after the ordinary shares had reached a cumulative dividend of £8 per cent per annum upon paid-up capital.

"This undertaking was received with satisfaction."

North Walbottle Village, 1942, taken from the 'Coronation Colliery' waste heap, behind Coronation Row, with Callerton Village in the background. The gap on the right is where a German plane dropped a bomb and three people were killed.

HOUSING AND STREETS

There are 5 maps available dated 1865, 1898, 1921, 1938 and 1970 which indicates the growth of the area we now know as Westerhope and District.

Details of the progress shown on each map are listed later, but meanwhile, the following is a list of dates applicable to Westerhope Village in particular:

1860:	Primrose Cottage was built
1890:	Buildings were commenced by the Northern Allotment Society (including Runnymede)
1900:	24 houses to their specification were completed
1901:	Westerhope Church built (60 adults and 12 children attended)
	Boyd Terrace built
	Rogerson Terrace built
	Belmont Cottages commenced
	Beaumont Terrace commenced
1909/10:	Bainbridges Buildings commenced: comprising Lily, Mary and Edna Terraces (named after Jim Bainbridge's daughters)
	Montague Buildings – Thomas and James Streets (Benson's Buildings) and Denton Grove commenced
1924:	Windsor Crescent commenced
1928:	Ellesmere Avenue commenced
	Greenfield Avenue commenced
1929:	Methodist Church Hall built
1930s:	Garthfield Crescent commenced
1935:	Chatsworth Gardens commenced
	Matlock Gardens commenced
	Buxton Gardens commenced
	Bournemouth Gardens commenced
	Lynden Gardens commenced
1949:	Dilston Drive built (on completion of Dilston Drive there were 1,012 houses in Westerhope).
1957:	Hillhead Estate commenced
1963:	Chapel House commenced
	Newbiggin Hall commenced
1964:	Pilton Park commenced
	Woburn Way commenced
1968:	West Denton Estate commenced
1970:	Chapel Park commenced
1976:	St John's Estate commenced
1980s:	Rosemount commenced

In recent years West Meadows, Westwood Court and Chapel Grange have been built. The shopping centre at Chapel Park has been replaced by Hartburn Close.

In these few lines a tremendous history is gathered together, each with its own particular story to unfold.

North Avenue and West Avenue and indeed others are not listed. They were like Topsy – they just growed! Each of the avenues had some lovely quaint dwellings and the original streets, rightly called Clarty Avenues in the early 1900s and since! There is that lovely avenue of houses Highfield, typical of the dwellings intended to represent Westerhope as conceived by the Northern Allotment Society

Primrose Cottage, built in 1860, remains as a lovely reminder of the Red Cow Farm Estate which played a great part in the unfolding of the place we now have fond memories of – Westerhope.

*Above: Chatsworth Gardens –
the flood of June 1941. Boats
from Leazes Park were
brought here to take food to
stranded residents of
Chatsworth, Matlock and
Buxton Gardens. The fire
engine pumped the water
away down Stamfordham
Road.*

*Right: Bungalows on West
Avenue – Nos 150 and 148.
The entrance to Rosemount
Estate on right.*

*Left:
Highfield
Road –
Typical of
the heavy
snowstorms
of 1941 and
1947 with
snow
several feet
deep.*

Now to the progress indicated on those early maps:

1865: Existing –
    Butterlaw Farm
    Whorlton Hall
    Whorlton Grange
    Gingling Gate
    Red Cow Farm
    Hillhead Farm (Newburn)
    Black Swine Farm
    Peck's Houses
    Walbottle Colliery
    Blakelaw Smithy
    Newbiggin Hall

1898: Additions –
    St John's Church
    Whorlton School
    Gingling Gate Smithy
    Primrose Cottage
    Runnymede
    Cheviot View
    York Cottage
    Swiss Cottage
    Derwent View
    Highfield
    Kendal Green East & West

1921: Additions –
    North Walbottle Colliery
    North Walbottle Village
    St John's Vicarage
    St John's Hall
    Coley Hill Farm
    Westerhope School
    Harris's Nurseries
    Picture Theatre
    Chapel House
    Northumberland Gardens
    Montagu Colliery
    Westerhope Village

1938: Additions –
    Runnymede Public House
    Miner's Cottages
    Golf Course
    Windsor Crescent
    Ellesmere Avenue
    Greenfield Avenue
    Garthfield Crescent
    Chatsworth Gardens
    Matlock Gardens
    Buxton Gardens
    Bournemouth Gardens
    Lynden Gardens

1987: Additions –
    Dilston Drive,
    Hillhead Estate
    Whorlton Grange
    Chapel House Estate
    Newbiggin Hall Estate
    Pilton Park
    Woburn Way
    Rosemount
    Redburn Industrial Estate
    Mother's Pride Bakery
    Chapel Park

Since these maps were published, other building has taken place, but as we are relating to the maps in particular, these are not listed here.

Below: 'The Iron Man', Stamfordham Road, early 1900s. Runnymede and Denton Grove are in the background. The Iron Man was the gents' toilets – adjacent to the van.

14

JOE ALLISON

By 1914, my father's turn for a colliery house came round. We moved from a rented house at the east end of the village to the west end, right into the heart of the pit houses. No 11 Rogerson Terrace was to be my home until I was married in 1936. North Walbottle colliery houses consisted of Beaumont Terrace, a double row of 119 houses, Rogerson a row of 12 houses and Boyd Terrace, 9 houses.

At the top end of Beaumont Terrace stood a group of 32 stone houses which belonged to the Montagu Colliery. The village I knew as a child had been completed in 1912 and there was no more building until the middle 1920s when Newburn Urban District Council came and built council estates. Now by this time, mining families from both the "Monty and our pit occupied most of the housing in the village. The mixture of the two pits caused a problem or two in the ensuing years. I remember pitched battles between groups of "Monty" lads and lads from our pit houses. It became so bad, that people had to board up their windows. That sort of thing died out in the First World War, but a certain rivalry prevailed for years, when we had to play them at football or cricket; they always ended up with a fight or being stoned away. I'm not sure whether that was a Catholic or Protestant clash or just natural rivalry between the two pits.

Joe Allison with the North Walbottle Branch Banner.

But peace came at last with a few inter marriages. I married one of them. From that first spate of building we now have our small Wesleyan Chapel, built in 1901, which soon had a Sunday School trip to Whitley Bay, involving nearly every family, and, on that day, turning Westerhope into a dead village.

The first football team, cricket club and bowls club had their origins at the Chapel, and later during the 1926 strike, we made our own tennis court behind the Chapel. In 1902 what was called the "Tin School" was built to serve a Primary School, the other boys and girls had to travel to Whorlton School or if Catholic, to Bell's Close, Lemington until Westerhope Council School was built.

Next came the Co-op, then Bainbridge's Buildings where I was born. In 1912, the Westerhope Picture Palace was built. All this played a great part in the life of the Village. The Excelsior Social Club also had come into being with its particular part to play. One of the most important days of the year was dividend day at the store. I remember helping my mother reckon up her store checks, and, with the balance sheet at her side, she knew exactly how much "divi" she was entitled to.

Often, when as children we asked our parents to buy us something, the reply would be, "We'll see when the ship comes in." "Divi" day was one day when the ship did come in. The Picture Palace not only catered for our village, but others around us. Matinees every Saturday and holidays, showing our favourite stars – Tom Mix, Buck Jones, W.S. Hart, Charlie Chaplin, Buster Keaton – two-part comedies (part two to be continued next week) as well as newsreels, serials and the big picture. 'Go As You Please' competitions were very popular, with plenty of local talent to compete, and the Treacle Bun eating contest caused a lot of fun. Buns dipped in treacle, strung across the stage, and with your hands tied behind your back – the first one to eat one, of course, was the winner.

The 'coming shortly' list was always interesting and I remember one of the first big western epics was on the list for months – *The Covered Wagon* – until word came through that one of the wheels had come off and never reached Westerhope after all. I remember one old lady always brought a raw onion when she came to the cinema. If the film didn't bring you tears, the onion certainly did.

When the local owner died, another proprietor came along, changed the name to "ORION", made a few changes, kept it going for a while, but, in the end, had to give in to the dreaded disease "BINGO".

Rogerson Terrace, our home, formed with Boyd Terrace and the bottom end of Beaumont Terrace what was locally called "The Square" and this became a natural arena. We had a street gas lamp there, we could play games both day and night; we had games for every season, marbles, cigarette card games, kites (home made), iron hoops or "gourds" as we called them. I think the American National game "Baseball" was pinched from us, but we called it rounders, then all kinds of chasing games, and others, which were more mischievous.

The First World War was upon us and I remember the night it got us up out of bed, and looking outside, the whole place was astir. Searchlights were in the sky and we could hear the drone of the Zeppelin engines, which had managed to get almost to Ponteland. Men were running around telling every one to put out their lights. Another time, we were coming out of school and a few of us followed the first Military Funeral we had seen go along to Whorlton Church. We were fascinated, seeing the coffin on the gun carriage and watching as the soldiers fired their rifles over the grave.

Then every street had its Armistice and Peace Parties, with children receiving appropriate mugs. The women folk

North Walbottle Miners' Picnic in 1960. First left is George Gunn; at the rear Dick Phillipson; and second right Mr Easten.

were marvellous when it came to arranging that sort of thing, being a mile or so from the pit, we were lucky. Nice open country and fields, walks surrounded us. Just over the main road we could start picking blackberries and mushrooms. In the fields in season; we could see partridge and pheasant, and the corncrake from our streets. Barn owls and bats were present among the small farms in the village. The hedgerows abounded with varieties of wild flowers, but many of the species of birds have been pushed further into the country by the building of the big estates we have around us now.

The Co-op butcher used to kill his own beast and, when a pig was killed, the bladder would be thrown out to us lads, blown up and used as a football. Then the women made their way to the store with jugs and cans for blood, from which our mothers made black pudding.

Popular features of our streets were the Packmen; most had their regular customers. There was one we called the one shilling man – one shilling (5p) for a pair of pit stockings, one shilling pinnies etc. Street entertainers were another feature. One old lady and gent came along and sang a famous old weepie "If you love your mother meet her in the sky".

Some of the hawkers that came around the village, were a curse to the men who had been on early morning shift and were trying to get an afternoon sleep. The Vinegar and Pickles man with his monotone voice "Pickles, two pence a pint vinegar!" and rag men blowing their bugles, every tune from the post horn gallop to reveille.

Weddings and funerals had their particular customs. We loved weddings because there was always money to scramble for. We would encircle the wedding and chant "Hoy a ha'ppenny oot, me fathors in the spoot an aa cannit get him oot". It didn't happen very often, but if there was no thrown-out money, our chant would be "Shabby Wedding". Lovely black horses pulled the hearse and cabs at funerals. When the death happened, neighbours pulled down their blinds in sympathy, and didn't draw them until after the funeral. When the day of the funeral was known, "bidders" would come from different homes giving an invitation to all to attend. If the funeral was that of a child, young ladies would walk in front wearing a sash over their shoulders. The ladies would carry a baby's coffin. Men of the same size among the neighbours were picked as under-bearers and bowler hats and dark suits were the order of the day. This sometimes caused a problem. Some men had to borrow a "dut" but if no dark suit, a black armband was worn. I've seen hundreds of people walking behind the cortege, and maybe to Lemington, which is about two miles away. Mourners stood at the graveside (rain or shine) until the last sod was laid. Back home again, and the ladies would bring drinks out for the drivers of the cabs and hearse.

Then we had the christening custom, with the Godmother carrying the baby. If the baby was a girl, the first boy they met was presented with a small parcel from under the baby's shawl. This contained a piece of cake, a sandwich and a gift of a silver 3d or 6d. If it was a boy, the first girl seen got the parcel.

One of the sad sights in the village, was the number of men and lads who has been injured at the pit. The spinal injury was common, then that dreaded eye disease "Nystagmus", which was prevalent when the oil lamp was being used and forced many men into light jobs on the surface. The electric lamp did curtail that disease.

The Miners' Welfare Institute (The Tute) was built in 1926 with assistance from striking miners. It is now owned by Newcastle City Council and is managed by the Westerhope Community Association.

The day the council midden men came into our street was a very unpleasant occurrence. We liked to see their lovely horses, but there the joy ended. The contents of the old 'netties' being raked out on to the footpaths, the coming of the wash away toilet seemed like a miracle.

These were days when the washing day lasted nearly all day, with poss stick, tub and mangle. "Wesshin day" was the bane of the miner's life, and Joe Wilson's twin brother tells it all in a song. A stranger walking into any of our colliery houses would find the furnishings very much alike, the floor covered with "clippy mats", a double bed under the alcove of the stairs where our parents slept. A square table where we all had our meals. We had an oilcloth table cover for weekdays, but nice red plush one between meals on Sundays. A big coal fire, which called for constant black-leading and polishing. The mantelpiece usually had a type of chenille pelmet hanging round it, very often with "china dogs" on it. Also a brass fender.

Upstairs we had two bedrooms, where we managed quite well, because our family consisted of three girls and three boys. I knew families who had to sleep head to toe.

Nowadays, you rarely see school lads wearing shorts. When I was at school, we either wore short trousers or corduroy knickerbockers. I started work before I got long trousers, and the first time out wearing them, the corner lads greeted me with "Aye Aye" Joe I see ye've gotten 'britched'".

When I started work in 1923, there were working pits all around in Throckley, Walbottle, Lemington and one in Bell's Close, which got the curious name of the "Moosie". It was said that the roof was so low that the mice had skinned backs. Wherever you went, "pitmen" could be seen walking to or from their place of work and as this was before canteens or pithead baths, you could see the state of their clothes. The conditions they were working in – they would be seen at all times during day and night. This meant the small tin bath would be hardly off the floor. The housewife and often a daughter were on the go from morning to night, preparing hot meals or "dadding" the pit clothes. Often the Sunday dinner was the only time the whole family would sit down together. That is why it was such an important meal.

I'm often amused when I read the descriptions of a miner. I never found the average looking miner; we had tall, short and thin, fat and bowlegged as this old story shows.

Every pit had its buzzer, and it's amazing the information it gave to the village. Ours blew the time for 8 am, 12 and 5 pm and everybody checked their clocks. It blew for the start of a shift, and the end of a shift. We had buzzers blowing all around us, and my father and older men could recognize most of them, even those coming from "ower the watter". We knew ours by the key or tone it blasted forth in. Workmates from Newcastle used to say they could hear it clearly from the Barracks. It was nice to hear them blowing the old year out and the New Year in. Ours did that for the last time when it blew in the year of 1968.

The most ominous time at our pit was 8 o'clock at night. Three separate long blasts told us that the pit was idle next day. That would be for various reasons, such as slack time, but the most dreaded meant there had been a fatal accident, and the pit, as was the custom, would be idle next day as a token of respect. If a

Joe Allison, Desmond Walton – Founders of Westerhope Local History Society and co-authors of 'Bygone Westerhope', displaying the book.

workman was killed during any shift, the pit was "loosed" out for the rest of the day. The next pay day, each man gave a shilling for the benefit of the widow or the stricken family. A common belief among miners and their women too, those serious accidents came in three's. That kind of talk could be heard right round the village. Strangely enough, that sequence did frequently happen.

Now for something which affected the livelihood of most of the mining families in the village. This was before new working systems, and guaranteed wage agreements came along. Conditions in the pit for the piece worker, varied from one man's working place to another, which meant one man could work twice as hard for less pay than the man next to him who had a good working place. So the most important day for the miners and his family, was the day the cavils were drawn. (A 'cavil' was simply the working place of the piece worker.) Cavilling day came round at the end of three months or quarter. All piece workers' names were put into a hat or basin and, as they were drawn out, the name was placed beside a corresponding list of cavils or working places. So what ever sort of cavil a man got, good or bad, he had it for three months. To a family man, a good cavil meant he would be able to feed and clothe them much easier. If he drew a bad one, life still had to go on, but his wife would have a much harder time making ends meet, with a smaller pay packet. The newly married couple setting up, and the young lad courting, thinking of marriage, were all waiting anxiously for the results of cavilling day. If a man said, "aave gettin' a piano flat" that meant he had a good cavil, and the man who was unlucky would say "aal just manage to buy the bairn a new bonnet".

There were two superstitions attached to cavilling day, which were supposed to bring good luck. First, our mothers would have the young ones stand on their heads. I can imagine a good few upside down children in the village on that day of destiny. The other customary saying was "We'll hev to put the cat in the oven". I don't think that would be put into practice.

Here are a few more superstitions connected to the mining village. If he met a cross-eyed woman on the way to work, it meant he was going to have a bad day. If he had forgotten something after leaving home, it was considered bad luck to turn back.

Friday was the unlucky day down the pit, and if you put your shirt on inside out, you never had to change it. It was bad luck if a black cat crossed your path, but if it followed you, it was good.

I would like to tell you how our pit finished. By the middle 1960s, we knew North Walbottle colliery was on its last legs; the writing was on the wall. We were the only pit working for miles around and coalfaces were being worked just to keep us in work. Travelling time underground to our work, was taking up to an hour or so of our shift. To make it easier to reach coalfaces, the NCB sank a drift at Ludwick, between Black Callerton and the airport. We were then transported from the pit to the drift. When we heard men were to be sent to our pit from Prudhoe and Wylam, we weren't happy; we argued it would hasten the end for us. When our men were being transferred to other pits, they found the same feeling of resentment and integration problems. But when they got down to the Midlands, they found a different pit life. Machines doing all the work we were doing manually up here. They found seams of coal the height they had never seen before.

At our latest union meeting, when we knew the date of the

Joe Allison with wife Dorothy get ready to unveil the Millennium Clock Plaque with Rev. Wes Blakey looking on.

pit closure, we had voted on the question of who would be left at the pit on salvage. It was decided that a team of men who had been the longest at the pit should be chosen, and I was one of that team. The inevitable day came along, Friday, 23rd February 1968, when our pit was drawing coal for the last time. The following Monday, our salvage team were left with the two pits to ourselves, but on constant day shift, that was a change to going at one o'clock in the morning.

Our first job was to go to the far end of the pit to bring out water pipes, but our bother getting them to the shaft was of no avail, because they are still there yet, like a lot of other machinery.

During the weeks on salvage, we had time to natter and some were really heart to heart talks. "What are we going to do when we finished?" One said "Wor lass an me cud nivvor set a leek at each other aal day". On Friday 4th April 1968 we all rose up the shaft for the last time and, for most of us, the following week was to be the last as miners. That last was spent clearing the timber yard. The weather was glorious. We all agreed it was the most enjoyable week we had ever worked at the pit. The birds never sang sweeter, and I will never forget the look of relief on my wife's face when I went home from the pit for the last time.

ST JOHN'S CHURCH

The first church to be built in the area was the Anglican Parish Church of St John's, often called Whorlton Church. It was built in 1866 as what was termed a Chapel of Ease. It consisted of a nave and chancel with rounded apse built in plain stone to seat 200 persons. Formerly, parishioners had to travel to Newburn for worship at the church of 'St Michael and All Angels'. It is an old church, one of its records stating that in 1731, new stocks were erected for the Parish at a cost of 3 shillings and 8 pence.

St John's Church of England, built in 1866. Note the bell tower and rounded apse. This view was taken before the graveyard was established.

Most of the expense of building St John's was borne by Messrs. Spencers of Newburn Steelworks, and the foundation stone was laid by Miss Spencer of Whorlton Hall and Michael Spencer was presented with a silver trowel on the occasion.

The Parish celebrated the 50th anniversary of the reign of Queen Victoria on June 27th 1887, when a dinner was arranged by Thomas Spencer. A whole Ox was roasted and over 500 parishioners were entertained, each receiving two glasses of ginger beer or, alternatively, if preferred, lemonade. Tea was provided later with entertainment until 8 pm when a bonfire was lit on the high hills, followed by a fireworks display.

There was a great need for premises to cater for social activities; Sunday School, Mothers' Union meetings etc, and so in 1897 a hall constructed of corrugated iron, was erected alongside the church. This was intended as a temporary measure but it lasted for 77 years until rust took over. In November 1974 a new Church Hall was opened with all of its modern facilities.

In 1908 the Spencer family added an organ chamber to the Church and also paid for an organ to be installed by Messrs. Harrison and Harrison of Durham. Mr. John Spencer was to have been present at the opening but, alas, he had died and was buried on the day of the opening. The first use of the organ could have been at the funeral of this very generous man. Later in 1911, a new chancel organ chamber and vestries were added. The Harrisons transferred the organ to its new chamber and, again, the cost of these additions was the gift of the Spencer family.

At this time it was intended to demolish the nave and build a new one, with an aisle to the scale of the new chancel. It was not until 1959 that the old organ chamber was converted into a children's chapel and was dedicated to the memory of Rev. W.B. Watts, by the Bishop of Newcastle. The nave was and still is left untouched.

One of the most important changes in the history of St John's was when it became the new Ecclesiastical Parish in 1899, when the boundaries included High Callerton, Callerton, Black Callerton, East and West Whorlton and the hamlets of Butterlaw, North Walbottle and Westerhope.

There is no documentary evidence showing when the graveyard was established, but it seems to have been in the early 1900s. The graveyard was closed for burials on the 9th June 1976 with in excess of 1240 burials having been registered.

Plans have been prepared in 2010 for a complete redesign and refurbishment of the churchyard.

The Church with newly erected Church Hall in 1897.

THE METHODIST CHURCH

There were only a few homes in Westerhope before the turn of the century but, in those early days, Methodism was established in the village. During 1899 meetings were held in a stone cottage in North Avenue by Mrs. R. Wakinshaw, Mrs. J. Clark, Mr. W.W. Reay and Mr. J.D. Turner. The venue was then changed to a house in Highfield Road and then to Kendal Green, where a room was furnished with a pulpit and other church furniture, until the original Methodist Church was built in 1901.

The foundation stones of the Church were laid by the founders on 7th September 1901 and on the first Sunday in December, of the same year, the Church was opened, becoming part of the Elswick Circuit.

It was not long before additions were made to the original building. In 1905, the tower was built and the clock installed, in memory of former Alderman, T.R.Dodd, Commander of the 2nd Battalion, Railway Pioneer Regiment. This clock tower proved to be a popular landmark in the district.

By 1910, it was evident that the premises were too small, particularly with reference to the Sunday School. Accommodation was limited to 150, whereas there were 250 (1951) on the roll. Consequently, it was planned to add to the existing structure and, later in the year, foundation stones were laid and the extension completed.

Westerhope Methodist Church, in 1951 – with Church Hall built in 1929.

The Chapel Class Meeting in 1910. The original was held at Mrs Clarke's House "Kendal Green" before the Chapel was built. Standing: Mr. Findlay (Hepple's Farm), unknown, Thomas Houghton, James Pearson, Mr Reay (Black Swine Farm), unknown, unknown, Henry Alexander Hall, Mr J.D. (Piggy) Turner. Sitting: Miss Willins (?), unknown, Miss Clarke, Mrs Clarke (9 Kendal Green), Miss Lily Clarke (?), Miss Marion Whiteman, Mary Ann Mart.

In 1926 the Church was licensed for the solemnisation of marriage and, in 1928, due to the continued generosity of the France family of Newbiggin Hall, Mr. Gordon Dewhirst was appointed as the first Pastor of the Church. He served in that capacity for 20 years.

The Sunday School continued to flourish and, in 1929, the original hall was built to accommodate the Sunday School and to cater for entertainment and social functions.

The Church became part of the North West Circuit of Newcastle in 1933 and the old premises were completed in 1935, when the vestry was added between the Church and the Sunday School Hall. The Church celebrated its Golden Jubilee in 1951 when a Souvenir Handbook was published, containing many tributes to those who had founded and faithfully served the Church during its 50 years history.

Throughout the years, the Church has been responsible for all types of activities, both inside and outdoor, for all ages, and were instrumental in founding the Westerhope Cricket Club and Bowling Club.

Two of the social activities were outstanding – the 'Hello Gang' and the drama group – the 'Newhall Players'. They each gave a performance once a year, from Monday to Saturday, to packed audiences. They also gave performances at many other venues, such was their popularity.

Westerhope Methodist Church Hello Gang in 1954. Back row: Betty Spriggs, Eric Spriggs, Foster Wilson, Andrew Boyd, John Varty, Mary Sharp, Maureen Wood, Ernie Bell, Marion Taylor, Frank Peacock, Arnold Heppell. Front row: Shirley Howard, Jean Groom, Sheila Sharp, Marjorie Bell, Ethel Boyd, Jean Sharp, Dorothy Boyd, Sadie Hannant, Audrey Wrightson, Joyce Harrison.

In the early 1950s, estates were planned surrounding the original village and, to accommodate the increasing population, a building fund was launched with a view to building a new Church and Hall. Plans were prepared for the new complex but, due to lack of capital, it was decided to build the Hall; firstly, to suit Youth and Sunday School work, as the existing hall was now inadequate. Due to the generosity of the local community and the Joseph Rank and other trust funds, the erection of the Hall was commenced in May 1964 and completed in 1965 at a cost of £21,000 – a huge sum at that time!

Following the completion of the Hall, it was intended to relax for a while before commencing the building fund for the new Church. However, dry rot was discovered in several parts of the Church, including the main supporting structure of the clock tower. Despite expert treatment and advice, the Church life span was estimated at a maximum of seven years

Westerhope Methodist Church Football Team in 1959. Back row: Eddie Boyd (referee), Foster Wilson, Frank Peacock, John Whitfield, Robin Lyall, Rev. Sydney Tipping, Les Shotton, Robert Wilson, Harold Clarke (referee). Front row: Douglas Carrick, Peter Wilkinson, Rev Geoffrey Ferguson, Arnold Heppell.

Once again, the Church had to appeal to the generosity of the community and the Bank and other trust funds. It was decided to demolish the original premises to accelerate the efforts for the new and, coincidentally, the demolition commenced on 7th September 1972, precisely 71 years to the day after the foundation stone had been laid.

The foundation ceremony for the new Church took place on 9th June 1973, the stone being laid jointly by Miss M. Pearson and Mrs. M. Robson. They were the only remaining Church members who were present at the extension of the Church in 1910.

The Church was opened on the 30th March 1974 by the Rev. Arnold S. Johnson, a former Westerhope Minister. On the occasion, it was estimated that 700 people filled the Church and the Hall. It was a great re-union, many people having travelled considerable distances to be present on this splendid occasion.

The following is a list of Ministers who have served the Church so faithfully throughout its history.

1928-49	Pastor G.W. Dewhirst
1949-52	Rev. K. Wade
1952-54	Pastor M. Bradley
1954-59	Rev. G. Mills
1959-65	Rev. G.K. Ferguson
1965-72	Rev. A.S. Johnson
1972-79	Rev. G. Dougill
1979-84	Rev. G. Brigham
1984-92	Rev. D. Aldridge
1992-2000	Rev. W. Blakey
2000-06	Rev. J. McCleod
2006-08	Rev. P. Jackson
2008-	Rev. I. Suttie

Westerhope Methodist Church opened on 30th March 1974.

Other Churches for, which no historical details are available, were the Apostolic Church, which met in a corrugated iron hall at the end of Coley Hill Terrace in North Walbottle, and a branch of the Pentecostal Church which met in an upstairs room above the Co-operative Store, adjacent to Belmont cottages.

In more recent times, Anglican Churches have been built on Newbiggin Hall and Chapel House Estates and Roman Catholic Churches have also been built on each of the estates.

FARMS

Two of the village farms can be traced back to the mid 18th century when they belonged to the Montagu family of London and who also resided at Denton Hall – the present residence of the Roman Catholic Bishop of Newcastle and Hexham. They were the Red Cow and Black Swine Farms.

Red Cow Farm

This was situated at the foot of Beaumont Terrace, behind Rogerson Terrace in what is known locally as 'the Square'. No photographs are available of the farm. The farm's duck pond was reputed to be on the site of the Co-op Store and the farm hind lived in Primrose Cottage which was built in 1860 and still stands at the corner of Stamfordham Road and Newbiggin Lane.

Black Swine Farm

This farm existed at the junction of Stamfordham Road and Wellfield Lane at the outgoing end of Westerhope towards Newcastle. The original farmhouse still exists and has recently been refurbished and extended for a private dwelling, with additional modern houses being built on the site.

In the early 1900s, the farm was owned by the Reay family. Several photographs of the farm and house are still available.

Hillheads Farm

Originally there were two farms at Hillhead, one on the Newburn side and the other on the Denton side of the road. The only remaining part of the Denton Hillhead Farm is the old farmhouse, which is used as the Boy Scouts' Headquarters, whereas the Newburn Hillhead Farm was still in use in the 1980s. Its history spanned 500 years and, for a considerable period, was owned by the Arthur family. When Bobby Arthur died in the 1980s, most of the land was sold for private housing developments, but the original farmhouse and stone cottages have been retained.

Black Swine Farm at the entrance to Westerhope Village.

Turner's Farm

This farm was located in the centre of the village in North Avenue, until it was sold to property developers in the mid 1960s, when Woburn Way and adjacent houses were built on the site. This farm was mainly for cattle and pigs with large grazing areas. Because of the pigs, the farmer was affectionately known as "PIGGY TURNER" and was the Northern Allotment Society's Secretary and a prominent

Mr Arthur's Hillhead Farm from the South.

founder member of the Westerhope Methodist Church or Chapel as it was known when founded in 1901.

Varty's Farm

Varty's Farm was sited on West Avenue, the only part remaining being the family dwelling – the large stone built "Highfield House". This, like Turner's, was not an extensive farm and mainly comprised grazing land for their cattle, as they operated a milk business.

The house and land was later purchased by the Lowrison family who developed a market gardening business.

Above: The Varty family. Back row: Walter, Albert, Wilf, Jim, Laurie. Front row: Margaret Frank Mary, Herbert Annie Maggie, William Costantine and Lizzie Ellen.

Left: Highfield Farm attached to Highfield House, West Avenue. Edward (Teddy) Varty on horse back. Uncle Jim Varty at entrance to byre (cow shed).

Robson's Farm

On a much smaller scale, Robson's had several cows in a grazing area in North Avenue and they also had a milk business. The family lived in Lynden House in Lynden Gardens.

John Robson of Emmerson House, now Lynden House.

MARKET GARDENS

The following were Market Gardens in Westerhope:

Harris's – Stamfordham Road
Edmundson's – Stamfordham Road
Holdsworth's – West Avenue (1903)
Armstrong's – West Avenue (Park)
Finlay's – Rosemount (taken over by Holdsworth's)
Dicky Rowe – West Avenue (1902)

In their original assessment of the area, the NAS had reported that it was ideal for gardening with excellent soil and a good supply of water. It was no surprise that very soon, market gardens were developed.

A Mr. Edmundson owned the market garden next to the "Runnymede" but was eventually purchased by George Harris who founded Harris & Sons of Pilton Gardens. George was previously employed at Kew Gardens, London, and was one of the horticulturists involved in writing a book on the propagation and cultivation of rubber trees.

Tomatoes and spring flowers were the principal products of Pilton Gardens and, during the War years, tremendous queues assembled along Stamfordham Road for his excellent tomatoes, which were also marketed in South country shops.

Pilton Nurseries, Stamfordham Road. In the photograph is Pilton House, Mr Harris's home, and garden with extensive green houses taken from Newbiggin Lane, near Stamfordham Road.

Upon George's death, his son Arnold continued in the business but eventually sold the land to the builders, Messrs. J.T. Bell. who built the Pilton Park Estate in 1964.

Holdsworth's Market Garden, West Avenue, taken a month after closing. It was the last Westerhope Village market garden and famous for Westerhope tomatoes all over England.

Holdsworths started their market gardens in 1903 on West Avenue and later took over the gardens of Finlay's, which were next to them. They had a large area of greenhouses and, like Harris's, grew tomatoes and spring flowers. They also sold their land, firstly for the 'Rosemount' development and finally for the Bakery and Berkshire Close.

Dicky Rowe's cottage was built on West Avenue, near the top of Beaumont Terrace, in 1902, next to an old quarry. He developed his gardens and greenhouses at the rear of the cottage and worked these until old age took over! He lived in the cottage until he died in the 1980s.

The cottage has been refurbished and extended and has been transformed into a very attractive residence.

The Lowrison family lived in Highfield House on West Avenue and had a market garden on what was formerly Varty's farm. They had specific means of fertilising the land which was responsible for a plague of bluebottles in the 1950s. It was dreadful!

Dunford's Market Gardens staff, November 1979.

Armstrong's had gardens on the area – now occupied by the bowling greens and tennis courts –'Westerhope Park' but little is known of their business activities

Roger Dunford's was the last of the market gardens. He had a smallholding below the Black Swine, but the land was required for the Western Bye-Pass, so he transferred to a large site opposite the Jingling Gate. It was a very successful enterprise, but when it eventually closed down, it became the site for the West Meadows housing development.

Thomas Anderson at Harris's greenhouse situated at the rear of the Picture House. The site is now the Co-op Funeral Services, Newbiggin Lane. The photograph was taken from Stamfordham Road.

SCHOOLS

The first school in the area was at Black Callerton but no records are available regarding it's origin or of the number of children attending the school.

The first Board School in the district was Whorlton School, situated in a quiet country lane between St. John's Church and Butterlaw Farm. It was believed to have been built in 1874 but in an old paper, printed in 1887, it was stated that a 'Whorlton Presentation' had been made by Mr. J. Spencer to Rev. C.A. Fox, who had served 16 years as Clerk to Whorlton School Board, at the same time as he was officiating Curate of St. John's. This establishes the date of the school back to 1871. It was built for 110 children and pupils attended from Black Callerton and surrounding areas, some having to walk as far away as Luddick, near the Wheatsheaf Inn on the Ponteland Road.

Whorlton School the first school in the area built in 1874. Mr Baxter the first Headmaster, with Mrs Baxter and school staff are in the right side background. Note all the boys wearing caps and knickerbockers.

Between 1871 and 1894, the school had two elderly headmasters but in 1894 a young headmaster was appointed with a salary of £90 per year, with his young wife receiving £10 per year to teach needlework. At a later date she was appointed to the permanent staff.

When the Newburn Vicar, the Rev. Blackett Ord paid his first visit to the school, he remarked how young she was to be 'mistress of the house'. She and her husband – Mr. & Mrs. Baxter lived and taught there for the following 35 years!

The schoolroom was very large, with no partitions, with a spacious fireplace protected with a huge fireguard. This had its many uses – as the pupils had to walk long distances, often in bad weather, it was used to dry out their stockings (which

Westerhope Council School with Mr William D. Reed, Headmaster.

were threaded through the mesh) and then outer garments, which always took second place. When holes were noted in stockings or clothing, Mrs. Baxter saw to them being repaired in class – practical needlework.

There was no going home for lunch or school meals, so the pupils brought sandwiches; therefore, there was plenty of time for their clothes to dry before home time.

As miners were drifting into the area to

Westerhope Council School – pupils outside on Hillhead Road in 1910.

work at the new North Walbottle Colliery, some of them were unable to write, so evening classes were started to teach English, Writing and later Mining. It was at this time, 1902, Mr. Robert Telford of Highfield House, Westerhope, was acting Clerk to the School Board. The younger children of Westerhope now had their own school building – a wooden hall with a metal roof, on the site of the Examination Board HQ on Wheatfield Road but the older children still had to attend Whorlton School. In time, Whorlton became overcrowded and arrangements were made for infants and some juniors to have their lessons in St John's Church Hall.

In 1907 Westerhope School was built on Hillhead Road for 320 mixed pupils, so pupils from Westerhope, who attended Whorlton, were transferred to their new school.

Westerhope Council School around 1920. Back row: Jim Mitchinson, Jack Smith, Jim Young, John Smith, Billy Pallister, Tom Stoker. Third row: Ernie Freestone, John Bowden, Bill Statham, Jim Tippins, Jim Ames, Milburn Stokoe. Second row: Billy Sinclair, Henry Smith, Harold Robson, Joe Tarvis, Les Mackay, Jack Wood. Front row: Jarta Bocking, Joe Allison, Harold Rowntree, Tucker Soulsby, Jim Hume, Bob Smith.

The school's first Headmaster was Mr. Ramsay, who only stayed for a short while, being replaced by Mr. T.E. Herdman who, on retirement, was succeeded by Mr. W.D. Reed, who was respected by everyone in the neighbourhood. In addition to his school duties, he was actively interested in Church and social interests and conducted both St John's Church and the Methodist Church Choirs.

In 1910, an additional school was built on an adjoining site and Miss Bean was appointed as its first Headmistress.

The school also acquired additional land for gardens and playing fields. In more recent times other school buildings have been erected on part of this land.

Whorlton School has now ceased to function as a school and the building is under private ownership.

These schools were the forerunners of the tremendous advances made in the educational system. No leaving school at 14 years of age now, and the number of types of schools – too numerous to mention.

Sadly, the old school was demolished in the summer of 2003 (almost a century after it was built in 1907) and has been replaced by a modern single storey building with everything incorporated under one roof.

The new Westerhope First School was officially opened by David Bell HMCI on 15th July 2003. It became Westerhope Primary School following the reorganisation of schools in the Outer West.

Westerhope Council School – lessons in gardening around 1920. Mr Herdman, Headmaster, is wearing the trilby. Fourth from the left is Henry Smith, sixth from the left, Joe Allison, seventh from the left is Harold Robson.

Westerhope Council School football team in 1939. Back row: Mr J. Laider, (Farmer) Grey, Joe Proud, Phil Sharp, Mr W. Reed. Middle row: Arnold Bradley, Alan Phipps, Billy Inchmore, Jimmy Patterson. Front row: Fred McKillup, Robert Phillipson, Robert Cole (captain), George Williams, Joe Brown.

DOROTHY ALLISON

I was born at Scotswood as near to the Tyne as was possible and nearer again to the "View Pit", the scene of the Monty Disaster. I was the seventh child of a family of nine boys and four girls. We then lived in what was known as the "Pit Bank". I was one month old when we moved to Westerhope, to the colliery houses, which were owned by the Montagu Colliery, the owner then being Mr Benson. Thus our houses, which consisted of 32 stone houses in blocks of 4, were known as Bensons Buildings. We had no numbers on the doors then, and it wasn't until I was in my teens that they got street names – Thomas Street, James Street and West Avenue – and numbers, our house being No 11. I remember my mother telling us how she hated it, as our view was so different to what she had been used to. She was now looking into someone else's houses as we lived in a middle block, whereas before she had the Scotswood Dene and of course, overlooked the Tyne. However, it proved in the years ahead to be a lovely friendly community. We had quite a lot of Irish people as our neighbours and very good and kind neighbours they were too.

Well, as I remember, there seemed to be something special on everyday of the week. My mother was a semi-invalid, but every day she made sure that there was a different job that had to be done. I, being the youngest girl, left school before I was 14 years of age, to take over most of the household jobs that were to be done. My other sister, being an apprentice dressmaker, hadn't to dirty her hands, the other two sisters worked on the colliery farm.

Our house had a very big living room, with the big black fireplace with a boiler at one side and the oven at the other. The boiler had to be filled about three times a day, so there was plenty of hot water for baths for those working on different shifts, as there wasn't such a thing as a bathroom. My mother never had an alarm clock.

My father was a deputy at the pit. My eldest brother was married at the time I left school, but I had a brother, a putter down the pit, another brother an electrician at the pit, one a painter and decorator, and the other a clerk at the Education Office.

Every Monday morning, my mother would sit at the big square table, the one we used to have our meals on Sunday; the other oblong table was used for weekday

Dorothy Allison with daughter-in-law, Yvonne, granddaughter, Melanie, and grandson, Craig, at a Church Flower Festival.

meals and she would have all the navy blue Sunday suits that the lads wore on Sundays, and she would brush them and fold them to be put away in the "Tall Boy Drawers", as we didn't have a wardrobe, until they were needed again.

Monday was the day when the vinegar man used to come. He shouted from the top of his voice, selling his pickles etc, much to the annoyance of the men who had been at the pit all night and were trying to get to sleep during the day. He would probably just get away when we should have the "Shields Kipper" man, who came regularly every Monday, calling "kippers two pence ha'pny a pair!"

Tuesday was the muffin man day, with the addition of countless ragmen and of course they blew their bugles to add to the noise. I always remember, as we came from school on Wednesday, what the menu would be for tea. It was always black pudding and white pudding and sausage fried (they call it grey pudding at our butchers now) as that was the day the butcher came with his cart and horse.

When I left Church Road School on the West Road, our washing day was a Wednesday – my mother would have no other day. As I have told you, the different jobs my brothers had, you may realise what a washing day was like and I was only 14 years of age. We didn't have a kitchenette or scullery, but we did have a big wash house attached to a very big pantry. We didn't have a tap inside either, as the tap was in the wash house.

We had two bedrooms, one a very large one with two double beds in for the lads and a smaller bedroom for the girls and a bed in the living room, where my parents slept. By now, two of my sisters were in domestic service, or as it was called then they were 'at place', so my washing day would start. A set pot was heated by a coal fire, a big poss tub and a big mangle. I had to wash big flannel shirts for my father, striped petticoats for my mother, pit clothes for one brother, greasy overalls for the electrician, white painter's overalls for the decorator and of course, always white shirts for the clerk. Our lads never ever wore any thing but white shirts and always shirts and collars had to be starched. My mother used to say coloured shirts were common. Plus, we had four beds going, so you can imagine the washing. No electric iron either, the old flat irons heated on a red hot coal fire summer and winter, and yet I enjoyed it and still do love a washing day.

Church School, West Road, near entrance to Denton Hall.

As I said, we had marvellous lots of good times with our neighbours – as children, we loved the weddings There was quite a lot or so it seemed to us. Many people kept pigs and it seemed there was always a pig killed in readiness, when there was a wedding. My mother used to keep all the potato peelings to help to feed the pigs and I suppose, we having a big family, there always was a lot of peelings to be collected. When the day of the wedding arrived, we would stand outside the house waiting for the bride to appear. As soon as she stepped into the cab we began chanting "Hoy a hapney oot" many a scraped knee we had, grabbing and knocking each other down for the sake of a copper. Sometimes, if they were well off, we might manage a "Threpney Bit".

I never knew any of our neighbours then, having a reception in a hall. The reception or tea was in the house, it was a real "Red Letter" day for us children. As all the children in the blocks were invited after grown ups had their tea, and then the fun started. They sat us on the floor in a ring and someone would come round with great big side plates of pork sandwiches. Then the dancing would start, some one would play a Melodeon, and the old Horn Gramophone would be on till 3 o'clock in the morning; and I am sure we children had we been allowed, would have stayed up until that time, because it sounded from our bedroom as if it went on all night and well into the week.

We also had a regular pack man who came once a fortnight – he would whistle all the time he walked up our garden path. We always knew him as "George the Jew". He was a lovely fellow, always well dressed. He used to call to my mother "Are you there Ma" knock on our door and come in. He always put two bars of chocolate 2d bars, one Cadbury's Nut and Milk and a plain milk bar onto the high mantelpiece, for my little brother. He would empty the contents of his case, pinnies, pit stockings, vests etc all at one shilling each. Sometimes my mother couldn't even afford anything to buy, but it didn't bother George, he would fold them neatly up and place them back.

I had an errand to make once a quarter when they paid the dividend out at the Co-op. That was the day when we felt we were in for a treat. I remember the time when we were paid the sum of 2/6 in the pound, that was the day my father got the big boost to his pocket money. My mother gave him an extra shilling, to put 6d each way on a horse, better still for him if he backed a winner.

One thing I did at that age, I certainly wouldn't have liked to do today, was when I was entrusted to collect from the Montagu Pit Offices 15 men's wages. I walked from Westerhope down to Scotswood one week on a Friday, the other on a Saturday. It was all fields right down across the West Road. At Denton Square I passed my old school. My mother used to give me a crocodile leather handbag and a big safety pin so I could fasten it up in the middle. I used to hand in the pay slips at the pay office. There was an electrician's, overmens, deputy's, coal fillers and hewers. I used to get 3d from each of them, which I was grateful for, but what a risk!

During the "Monty" Pit disaster, my father was one of the rescue team as he had worked all his life at the colliery. It was very sad for him as he knew every man. When he used to come home, my mother would tell us not to ask him any questions, and we didn't. I can remember the terrible smell of his pit clothes as he came home after being on that awful job. The first thing he used to do was to take them off and throw them in the back yard, and then clean ones had to be ready for him for the next day.

A pleasant thing to remember was the Methodist Chapel. I was christened and

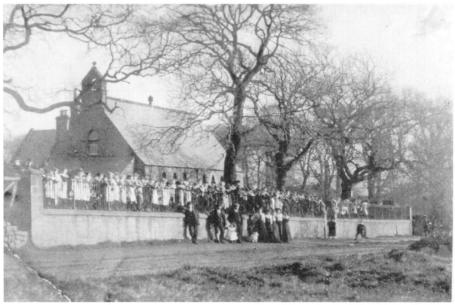

Church School, West Road, in the early 1900s. Near to entrance to Denton Hall and Denton Square, pupils from Westerhope walked to attend this school prior to 1907.

confirmed an Anglican, but the parish was out of the village at Whorlton and the chapel was in the centre of the village. We had all our entertainment there; we had magic lantern shows and socials, where instead of paying a 1d or 2d to go, we were asked to take an apple or an orange; these were cut up and put into a big dish and, at the interval, was passed around for us to take our choice.

Of course the highlight of the whole village was the Sunday School trip. For a lot of years we walked down a mile or so to Kenton Station where the Metro Terminus is now. It was a day when the village emptied, all the parents went, because then I think all the children went to Sunday School. We had games on the sands, and there used to be as many drunken fathers as sober ones, but it was something to have all the families together. It was lovely being at the seaside, but oh the walk coming back – how we wished that train would continue up the bank to Westerhope. As the years went by, the buses became popular. There were times when there were 12 double-decker buses, and then of course the motor cars took over and the Sunday School trips to the seaside finished. Rather a shame I think.

SHOPS

In the early days, Westerhope residents depended on horsedrawn travelling shops to supply their groceries, general supplies and paraffin oil for lamps etc. There was Mr. Wanless, Mr. Green and a Mr. Roy from Blackfriars. He was a really enterprising man! People wondered why he carried a basket on the back of his cart, it actually held

pigeons. When he received an order from a house, he wrote it on a slip of paper, put it in a ring, attached it to the pigeons leg and sent it winging back to Blackfriars, where they received the order, packed it up, ready for Mr. Roy to deliver it earlier than other carriers could manage.

Other local carriers followed such as Mr. W.J. Anderson (the originator of Anderson's Buses) and Mr. Close of Westerhope. However, as the village developed in the early 1900s, several shops were opened.

There was Tom Bell's shop (now Barclay's Bank) where you could buy virtually anything, including pick heads and other items for use underground. At the opposite end of Belmont Cottages was Davidson's the butchers shop. It was later occupied by Allan's Stores, managed by Rachel and Lena Wilson and eventually owned by them. Ownership then came to the wine merchant Augustus Barnett. At present in 2010 it is unoccupied and up for sale.

Mr & Mrs Tom Bell in the early 1920s. Tom built this shop and the adjacent terraced houses, giving them the name Belmont Cottages. His shop is now the premises of Barclay's Bank.

Mrs Allen outside her shop at North Walbottle. Her son Jack scored the two goals for Newcastle United when they won the FA Cup Final in 1932, when they defeated Arsenal by 2 goals to 1.

The present Chemist's shop was firstly occupied by the Close family, a general dealers, who also operated the carrier business between Westerhope and Newcastle. The first baker in the village was a Mr. Clough, followed by Teasdales with the bakery now owned by Thompson's. Wightmans were the first Chemists, operating from a stone built house on Stamfordham Road. Passers-by were intrigued by the figure of a white horse in the window, which they eventually discovered, proved that he was a qualified vet. Watson's had a general dealers shop in the present Estate Agency on Stamfordham Road. Paddy Wanless, the travelling dealer, started a clothiers business on the site of Armstrong's Garage.

It was a big event when the Throckley Co-op opened a branch in 1908 at the junction of Beaumont Terrace and Stamfordham Road and the start for many of 'dividend' days. Opposite the Co-op, Ella Hart had a newsagent's business. Next to her shop was Whittey's confectioners and barbers shop with Arthur Hall, cobbler and local historian around the corner, still known as 'Cobblers Corner'.

Left: Mr E. Hart's – first newsagent in village – Ella Hart is in the centre. The shop was near the junction of Newbiggin Lane and Stamfordham Road.

Right: G.G. Hancock, newsagent & confectioner's, Stamfordham Road in the 1930s. Doris Hancock is at the door of her father's shop talking to a customer.

Mr. John Dickinson, the dairyman, lived on the corner of Newbiggin Lane and Stamfordham Road and also owned the section of land at the rear where he trained racehorses. On West Avenue, there were several general dealers – Anderson's, Dick Green, Arthur Hall, Brown's and Mrs. Ostell with her house shop.

In North Avenue, there was a house shop owned by Bill Allison (father of local historian Joe Allison). The Stanley family also had a house shop in Stanley's Buildings and Mrs. Powell sold pies and peas from her house shop at the foot of North Avenue. In nearby North Walbottle, Mrs. Allen had a lovely house shop in Coronation Road with an outside platform for children to view the sweets in the window. Mrs. Allen's son Jack scored the two goals for Newcastle United when they defeated Arsenal 2-1 in the 1935 Cup Final at Wembley.

In a recent survey by the History Society, they recorded that since the 1890s there has been a variety of over 70 shops established in the village.

Right:
429 Stamfordham Road, originally Davidson's the butchers who had a store built on a different angle from alongside Belmont Cottages. This was to avoid sunshine affecting the meat on display. It was eventually Allan's Stores followed by Augustus Barnett.

Ron Bould & Son – formerly Bright's Post Office – 1978. It was at the corner of North Avenue and Stamfordham Road.

Lexia Foods in 1991. The proprietor was Mrs Anne Trotter and on the right is Ann Marshall. Anne is a committee member of the Westerhope Resident's Association and the Westerhope Community Partnership.

WESTERHOPE PICTURE PALACE

Paul Heslop, author and former Westerhope resident, shares his memories of the Westerhope Picture Palace – an article originally published in 'This England' magazine:

Westerhope Picture Hall was built in 1912 by Sam Piper and his sons, who were all miners at North Walbottle Colliery. It was indeed a palace as it was brick built and most of the others in the district were wooden structures.

It was called "The Orion", but sometimes we called it "Old Sam's" after the name of its owner. Mainly, though, it was "the flicks" or "the pictures", and, cruelly, "the flea pit". Whatever its name, it was our local cinema.

When we were young, the cinema was an important part of our lives. No-one had TV then, except, that is, the local Co-op, where we peered through the shop window at the flickering black and white picture on our way home from school. Sometimes we'd sneak into the shop for a closer look. Then we'd be able to listen, too, but such a privilege could last a few minutes only, for discovery would result in being ordered out.

My first memories of the Orion were as a young boy. I went with my parents, mainly. Dad liked Westerns; Mum's favourites were what were loosely described as "love stories".

When very young, I could not understand why cars on the screen drove on the opposite side of the road. Later, I could identify spelling mistakes in words such as "Technicolor". I was, of course, viewing American films.

Most communities had their own cinema in those days – not too close, not too far away. This meant competition for the Orion, but so many films were on in the course of just one week at each cinema, you could stick to one and still enjoy a varied selection.

There was a main feature on Monday and Tuesday, another on Wednesday and Thursday and another again on Friday and Saturday. There was yet another on Sunday. Each was preceded by a 'B' movie. Along with trailers (anything with Randolph Scott was a must) and advertisements, there would sometimes be Pathe News. Alternatively, Coal News would be shown, the latter a sort of propaganda production aimed (one supposes) at the locals, many of whom – including my father – were coal miners. Looking back, I wonder how he felt, watching miners drilling the coal face to the sound of music?

Old Sam's Picture House during the First World War. Here is a group of wounded soldiers from the Royal Victoria Infirmary. Sam Piper is in the centre.

Such was the popularity of the cinema, it was not uncommon for Old Sam's to be so packed that people stood in the aisles.

There would be no complaints about this, not from folk who were only too pleased to have got in. As I recall, the Orion bulged with people for *Ben Hur* and *The Ten Commandments*, while many other films also attracted large audiences.

If a really good film was coming, you had to book a seat. This meant visiting the home of the proprietor, Mr. Longhorn, where you were admitted into the hallway and your reservation carefully entered into a posh-looking book. How special you would feel on the night when the letter 'R' was fixed to the back of your seat. It was 1/6 or 1/9 for the rear stalls or the gallery. The latter seats were expensive and out of bounds to us, except for Saturday matinees when children could sit where they liked.

Sometimes we would go to the pictures on the first night and spend the second night outside, where we could hear the voices of our favourite stars booming out from the projector room.

Evacuees from London and pupils from Westerhope Council School outside the Orion Picture House during the Second World War.

As kids, our mischievous antics merited the closest scrutiny by Longhorn himself or, worse, by Doreen the usherette. Watching the film was only a part of our night's entertainment. Anti-social digressions were carried out with ruthless abandon to the annoyance of genuine cinema-goers – talking, calling out to friends, facing in the wrong direction and deliberately rustling crisp packets.

We'd blow into empty "pop" bottles, causing deep sounds to echo throughout the auditorium. Then we'd release the bottles onto the sloping floor, to roll and clank against the metal legs of seats. Sometimes we fired what appeared to be lighted matches into the lights of the projector. Longhorn would stop the film and threaten to throw everyone out. I swear he never realised they were only pieces of paper propelled from elastic bands.

There was, of course, the risk of identification, with ejection a likely result. Longhorn's approach however, was easy to detect, for the red glow of his cigarette and balding head (on which the light projecting from the screen reflected) gave away his presence.

Doreen was another matter. She could be secreted in the recess of a fire exit, or even seated surreptitiously on a row. She could tell from fifty seats away just who was doing what. Without moving position, she would chill the blood of the miscreant by screaming "Stop it!" followed by various threats of retribution.

Sometimes, someone in the gallery would walk in front of the projector, causing a gigantic, ghost like shadow to block out whatever drama was unfolding on the screen. This was a reason for feet stamping. For good measure, if the shadow wasn't removed quickly, there would be loud jeers and boos. Yet, despite our misdemeanours, no-one ever got into real trouble. No-one ever damaged anything, not once. Our antics were fairly harmless.

Saturday morning matinee compelled attendance to watch our cowboy heroes – Roy Rogers, Gene Autry and Hopalong Cassidy. There was Superman too and, of course, Tarzan. Then there was a serial about Nyoka, the Jungle Girl. I never understood why the same episode was shown every week. Nyoka was trapped in a room as water poured in. When death seemed certain, it ended. Perhaps she died in the next (unseen) episode and old Longhorn hadn't the heart to show it.

Everyone knew Roy Rogers' fourlegged friend was called Trigger, so he was the most popular cowboy of all. For some reason, I always remembered the name of Hopalong Cassidy's horse too. His name was Topper.

As Saturday's matinee finished, an observer at the doors of the Orion would have witnessed a horde of young boys, clad in short trousers, emerge from the building and gallop off in different directions. They'd be shooting at some "ornery critter" who, though unseen, would be returning fire. Sooner or later they'd dismount for the inevitable shoot-out. It was all good clean fun.

As we grew up, our attitudes changed. There were no more rolling bottles, no paper missiles. By mid-teens we went to the pictures either because a particularly good film was showing or, equally likely, it was time for another activity – girls.

A girl's acceptance of your invitation to the Orion held the promise of a new and exciting adventure. When the lights dimmed it was time to get on with the night's proceedings which, quite likely, was not to watch the film – not if you'd managed to book one of the special double seats at the back of the gallery.

With the absence of an arm-rest, you could get really close to your partner. Many people must have made their first romantic advances in the almost total darkness of the Orions of this country.

It mattered not that there might be a few hundred people present. Everyone else was either riveted to the actions of Errol Flynn or doing the same thing. Yet, when the film ended and the lights came on, everyone broke their loving embraces and nonchalantly looked to the front as though nothing had happened.

In later years, when other cinemas closed, the Orion somehow managed to survive, but then it too shut down its projector.

Today the Orion's still there, but now it's a Bingo Hall – just somebody calling out numbers. "Kelly's Eye" and "Legs Eleven". I'd never go there for Bingo. It just wouldn't be the same.

The former Orion Picture House on Stamfordham Road. Former miner, Joe Allison is standing in the entrance.

SOCIAL ACTIVITIES

It is amazing how people thought that life must have been dull before the advent of television, music centres etc. In the early days in Westerhope, people made their own entertainment. Children in particular had no problems. There was a wide variety of activities in which most children were involved some time in each day. We started before school time, on the way to school and during school playtimes. After tea, we played outside until we were reluctantly 'called in' by our parents for bedtime.

Adults too seemed to have plenty to occupy their leisure time. As mentioned earlier, the Church or Chapel were the source of most activities with social evenings, various mid-week meetings and people didn't just watch football and cricket matches, they were actively involved in them.

Westerhope had its own football, cricket, bowling and tennis teams and were proud of their sword dancers, who were champions, making professional appearances in the theatres in the 1920s all over Britain. Morris dancers performed the North Walbottle Sword Dance.

Westerhope Village Dance at the 'Tute'.

Quoits was always popular and it was not unusual to see men playing quoits and marbles alongside each other.

Choral singing and brass bands were enjoyed by many but another highlight was, as it is today, the pilgrimage to St James' Park to see Newcastle United. Boxing and wrestling on Monday and Saturday nights respectively at St James' Hall opposite the football ground was followed eagerly by those who could afford it. Although it only occurred annually, the Chapel Trip was possibly the most outstanding event of the year; yes, even more popular than the Cup Final!

In the early 1900s the trips to Whitley Bay went from Kenton Bank Station which is approximately two and a quarter miles from Westerhope. Everyone had to walk there. It was not so bad going there but after an active day on the beach and playground, everyone was quite weary when returning.

On arrival, most parents queued for tents and deck chairs. Whilst they were 'settling in' on the sands, the children would go to the show ground at the Spanish City or enjoy the 'Shuggy Boats' or donkey rides on the beach. After an early lunch of ham and egg pie and lettuce and tomato sandwiches, the programme was generally making sand castles for the competition, for which there were prizes, organised games by the teachers and the bathing or 'plodging' (paddling) for the rest of the day before tea time. Then the long trek home!

Eventually, the venue was changed to Tynemouth and the walk to and from Kenton Station was eliminated. We booked several double-decker buses for as little as £3 each, the buses leaving from and returning to the Chapel. The Sunday School scholars – three on one seat, travelled free, with non-scholars paying one shilling (5p) and adults two shillings (10p).

Jim Bainbridge (the man who managed the sinking of Walbottle pit shafts) his wife and other villagers, in a peace celebration in 1919.

Looking back, it was great fun, everyone joining in – almost every child carrying a bucket and spade and, some, fishing nets. The penny lucky bags we bought from the pedlars on the beach, ice cream cornets, candy floss etc.

Then there were mothers with long skirts or dresses, tucked up delicately, plodging in the sea and fathers with shoes, with laces tied together, slung over their shoulders as they plodged along too.

They were 'red letter' days in spite of sand in our sandwiches, in our eyes and in our shoes for several days afterwards.

When we extended our Sunday School to include Blakelaw children, meeting at Hylton School, they were invited to join us and, on one occasion, we had 15 double decker buses taking us to the coast. The area was like a ghost town.

This was the only day that some children ever saw the sea but how things have changed with the passage of time. When asking people these days where they are going for their holidays, the reply so often is in terms of 'we are just going to Majorca or Ibiza' etc.

Probably the most popular of all activities was cinema going. Visits to Newcastle cinemas and theatres were special occasions, but attending the local cinema, eventually called 'The Orion', is a separate subject in *Westerhope Remembered*.

Whippet racing – the miners' sport. This photograph was taken on the field adjacent to the Miners' Institute.

Westerhope Old Boys Football Team in 1944. Back row: Dick Clake, Syd Hewitson, Arnold Heppell (Junior Secretary), Jack Hancock, John Tulip, Jim Lumsden, Jack Laidlaw (Chairman), Stan Peacock, Fred Bewick (Committee Member). Second row: Ken Mole, John Lumley, Henry Taylor, Tom Peacock (Secretary), Frank Smith, Gordon Statham, George Steele, Bill Heppell, Maurice Reay, Norman L. Lumsden. Front row: Tom Brown, Tom Sparkes, Andrew Williams, Joe Brown, Raymond Robson, ? Stoker, Ron Steele.

Above: Westerhope Bowling Club – Tom Wheeler, Jack Hancock, Git Heslop. They all played for Northumberland County.

Playing tennis at Highfield Road – Mrs Wilkinson and Mr Wandless – in the early 1900s.

Right: Westerhope Golf Club was originally a nine-hole course founded by Newburn Urban District Council in 1941. In the 1980s it hosted the Variety Club Celebrity Golf Classic and sporting legends such as Bobby Charlton, Jackie Milburn and Henry Cooper tee-ed off here.

Westerhope Golf Club, Ladies' Day around 1950. Front row: Mrs L. Wilson, Mrs M. Embleton, Mrs M.M. Bell, Mrs M.E. Makepeace, Mrs J. Goodrich, Mrs K. Smith, Mrs G. Burrows. Second row: Mrs B. Nixon, Mrs E. Dack, Mrs N. Gill, Mrs F.E. Bird, Miss V. Wakenfield, Miss U. Garland, Mrs B.R. Weddell. Third row: Miss D.P. Ridley, Miss A. Milner, Mrs M. Dearing – above them: Mrs D. Carr. Fourth row: Mrs I. Wilson, Miss M. Purdy, Miss M. Costello, Mrs E. Nixon, Mrs M. Cuthbertson, Mrs N. Young, Miss L. Renwick, Miss W. Leslie, Miss B. Keen, Miss S. Adamson, Miss M. Lockhart, Mrs E. Brabazon, Mrs M. Shannon, Miss R Garland.

Stan and Tom Peacock leaving the third green.

A comprehensive history of the club is available in local libraries in a book by Colin Makepeace, son of the first professional of the club. Colin has been captain of the club on two occasions and has represented the County team as captain and was an England Boy International in 1953 and a Youth International in 1955 and 1956.

ANDERSON'S

Mr William John Anderson, father of the "brothers", moved to the north east of England from Scotland, first living in the Newburn area and then in what was to become Westerhope in the 1880s.

He laid the foundations of the Anderson business by starting with a horse and flat cart, trading in greengroceries around the area. Within a few years his eldest sons, John and William, joined him with more horses and carts and they began to transport goods such as corn and hay for the local farmers and bricks for the buildings that were being erected at the time.

In 1892 Mr Anderson bought a plot of land in Wheatfield Road, Westerhope, where he established his stables and built a row of six terraced houses. By this time younger sons Albert and Thomas were of an age where they were required to work in the business. Boys of 10 years old had to do men's work in those days.

With the help of his sons and hired hands, the business grew to having about 20 carts and 3 dozen horses. The lack of grazing for the horses became a problem and so a plot of land was purchased for this purpose. This was opposite the Picture Hall bordering Stamfordham Road and became what is now Chipchase Crescent. Later, a further plot of land was purchased opposite the Jingling Gate, where the estate now known as West Meadows stands.

Anderson's main business was haulage. Work came from a local quarry owned by a man named Elliot, the Kenton Quarry also providing lots of work. Anderson's led cut stone and loose stone for road works. Since the pit at North Walbottle had not yet started production, domestic coal was led from Kenton Bank Foot station. Other work came from leading heavy cast steel and metals, especially from Spencer's Steelworks in Newburn.

By 1903-04 the village population had grown tremendously and the family saw the need by the villagers, for transport into the city. They set about providing this service for them, running "brakes" to Newcastle. The

Westerhope Garage on Stamfordham Road in 1959 with a mixed fleet of Bedford B.M.C Leyland Vehicles. The site is now occupied by housing – Westward Court.

brakes were the flat four-wheeled carts used for haulage, but with a portable rig containing form-like seats bolted to them. The brakes only ran on certain days. Friday and Saturdays saw a regular service but a weekday service was only available if there was a need.

At this time, the topography of the local land was rather different than it is today, being nowhere near as flat. This created problems for the brakes. Most of the problems lay with the steep bank known as Heathery Shank Bank and the marsh ground between Silver Lonnen and the Black Bank leading to Black Swine Farm. To overcome both banks Mr Anderson negotiated a deal with the farmer who owned Heathery Shank Farm to allow him to keep six trace horses tethered, ready for use, to aid the four-in-hand horses up both banks. This saved the passengers having to alight.

Albert Anderson would recall that, as a 13 year old boy, he would haul stone and other heavy loads from the early morning until late evening, wash the cart down, manhandle the rig onto the cart, harness fresh horses and then pick up passengers for Newcastle. The last brake from Newcastle would leave at around 10 pm from Nelson Street. Albert amused us by saying it generally took 50 minutes to Newcastle but the horses would know when it was the last load and would return in 40 minutes. Often he could not see a hand in front of him due to fog coming up the Black Bank, so he just let the reins go and the horses picked out the tracks themselves. The driver's work was not finished until the horses were fed, watered and groomed, the rig removed ready for the next day's haulage and the horses led to the field to graze.

In 1907-8 the business bought their first motor vehicle with a manual type tipper. The next year they increased to three vehicles, again offering haulage by day and a passenger service in the evening. Competition, however, was looming in the shape of the Newcastle Corporation who was experimenting with a purpose built bus. Anderson's purchased two Daimler charabancs to head off the competition but by 1912, the Corporation had established a designated bus route from Newcastle to Whorlton Church, which put Anderson's out of service. They did however continue with the two Daimlers, offering private hire.

In August 1914, Albert Anderson was called up to the army. More devastating to the business, however, was that the War Department requisitioned all their vehicles for war service. It was back to the horse and cart for the duration of the war. On his return from the forces in early 1919 he found that the business had suffered due to loss of pre-war contracts. He also found that his father and brothers John and William were no longer interested in the business, so, together with brothers Thomas and Alex, who had been born in 1903, they formed the company of Anderson Bros (Westerhope) Ltd. There was great reliance on horse drawn vehicles to carry out the work they generated, production of new motor vehicles being slow to start up post war, but by around 1921, they had acquired a number of vehicles, including 2 new charabancs. Again work came from leading cereals from the farms and from North Walbottle pit, whilst quarry work and long distance work came from all over the country.

In 1923, Mr Anderson bought a house in Belmont Cottages from the Bell Family (next to Allen's Stores). He installed a gasoline pump in his front garden and supplied to the passing motorist. On a good day he could sell 10 gallons of fuel, there not being many cars around in those days! He had the pump removed in 1929. Also in

Bill Anderson & Sons – Westerhope Haulage Contractors – Albert Anderson, Tom Anderson, Alex Anderson and Bill Anderson, the father.

1929, the brothers bought a plot of land next to Piper's Picture Hall from Mr Harris and built three houses for themselves. By 1932 the fleet had grown to 25 lorries, mostly Bedfords. Horses had gradually been phased out over the years, but Albert had always been a horse man and, up until his death, people around the county sought his advice on horse matters. As a result of having no horses to graze, the fields opposite the picture hall became a row of 7 semi-detached houses, known as Kensington Villas.

The directors, who had hired Mr Favour to build their three houses, were so impressed with his work that he got the job to build Kensington Villas. Unfortunately, the fixed price job ran over budget due to the fact that the site lay on top of what is known as the Whin Dyke, a very hard rock formation which stretches up the north east coast of England and the foundation work cost a fortune. Mr Anderson always said that Kensington Villas had the best foundations in Westerhope Village. The Company also built their new garage at the west end of the plot in 1935-36. The other field opposite the Jingling Gate was sold off.

In 1939, once again war was to knock the business back. Whilst no lorries were requisitioned, the war department had first call on the lorries at any time. Additionally, no new lorries could be bought, nor spare parts obtained for the maintenance of the fleet. At the end of the war in 1945, the three brothers decided to call it a day and go their own way. Thomas Anderson went back to the coach business and registered the T & A Anderson Company, Alex Anderson went into the greengrocery retail field, and thus in 1946 Albert Victor Anderson became the sole owner of Anderson Bros (Westerhope) Ltd.

Albert, along with his son Thomas Cameron, found that they now had a fleet of 20 odd vehicles that had been devastated with war service and a "rob Peter to pay Paul" maintenance scheme. No new lorries were available, so they bought second-hand lorries to meet their haulage needs. Work was becoming plentiful but lorries were scarce to come by, so to obtain more lorries, Mr Anderson bought out Fosters Haulage of Corbridge. By 1953 the business had a fleet of 46 vehicles and business was booming, leading coal into the new power stations of Stella North and Stella South, Dunston, Sunderland and Darlington.

From the Durham and Northumberland coalfields, from Crook to Shilbottle, Anderson's had contracts to lead coal. Continuing to carry farmers' produce brought the Company into lime spreading. The government paid the farmers a subsidy to lime their fields, so Mr Anderson bought two lime spreaders from a Lancashire motor company. The spreaders were Canadian Fords and this new type of spreader was able to spread lime by the ton in minutes, with just the driver, rather than the old-fashioned way of a driver and two men on the back, spreading using large shovels. A subsidiary company was formed called Westerhope Suppliers Ltd with the purpose of supplying coke and coal to domestic customers. Since the factories were now producing motor vehicles, the fleet changed over to Leylands which suited the work carried out by the business and a second garage was built on the site to accommodate the extra vehicles.

In 1963 Albert Anderson died. He had always been known as a charitable man, donating to local causes and, as many people who had been members of local Scouts, Boys Brigades or youth movements will recall his generosity in providing lorries on a Saturday morning to take them to camp sites in the country

A Coronation Float in 1953. An Anderson Brothers float passing near Garthfield Crescent, going towards the centre of Westerhope.

and then bring them back with their equipment the next Saturday, has long stayed in their memories. The University Rag week always had two or three Anderson floats in their parade and on the day of the Queen's Coronation, three lorries were laid on for the parade through Westerhope. When the weather on the day of a national holiday held for the Coronation turned out to be foul, the organisers of the street parties in the Chipchase area, approached Mr Anderson for help. He called out a number of drivers to empty the garage of lorries, clean down and carpet the floors with tarpaulins and erect tables. The party and games went on until late evening.

After his death, the business went to Albert's only son Tom. Tom had worked in the haulage business all his life and was an expert in the field of transport. He was assisted by his two sons Albert and Paul who became managers and directors. Tom was well known in the village for his love of birds. He bred and raised rare birds but his forte was pigeons. As a member of the Westerhope Homing Society he won two national trophies in the same year – the HM The Queen's Cup and the Vaux Breweries Gold Cup.

During the 1960s, a third garage was built and equipped with modern workshops, road testing equipment, engine over-haul and tyre testing. New offices were also built.

In the period from the late '60s to the early '80s the directors changed the fleet to 38 ton Volvo vehicles. They also established a plant hire side to the business, operating tractors, earth moving equipment and bulldozers. At its peak, the business employed over 80 people. With the big fleet, Anderson's could negotiate big contracts. They hired small haulage contractors to sub-contract for them. Young Albert once mentioned that he had more lorries on contract than in his own fleet. A page from the company's Daily Record Book showed how the business was diversified over a day in 1972:

5200 tons of coal transported
480 tons of lime taken to Scotland and spread
Long distance lorries in Southampton, Bristol, Liverpool, Glasgow and Leeds
1 lorry loading in Newcastle for London
4 lorries required at North Shields quay to pick up sprats for overnight journey to Hull
40 tons of coal delivered to domestic customers
50 miners receive concessionary coal
1000 gallons of petrol sold on forecourt (a long way from the single pump in Belmont Cottages).

The garage personnel were busy overhauling lorries and building wagon bodies whilst the office staff was engaged on wages, accounts and records. Albert and Paul Anderson became board members of the Tyne Haulage Training Board which was set up to further educate drivers and mechanics. By 1980, the Volvo fleet was fitted with radio receivers controlled from the office. This proved to be very efficient, helping to establish where every vehicle was and enabling re-routing to be done at once. The miners' strike in the early 1980s was devastating. The fleet was employed on jobs other than colliery work, but no sub-contractors could be hired. After the strike, collieries started to close and domestic customers turned to gas central heating. On top of this, the European Agricultural Policy had a major effect on the farmers. They lost the government's subsidies and so did not require lime. Their output was also greatly reduced. Additionally, long distance haulage was changing over to containerisation.

By 1996 Anderson's had to make decisions and, after exploring all the ways that the fleet could be used, the directors decided that the best way forward was to withdraw from the transport side of the business and to diversify into other activities. The last big red lorries of Anderson Bros (Westerhope) Ltd were seen on the roads of Westerhope in March 1996.

FOOTNOTE: Over a span of 100 years, Anderson's of Westerhope had become a major road transport contractor to the Northumberland and Durham coalfields.

Apart from railway freight, the only other main movers of coal from the area were the sea-going colliers. It is rather ironic that, two years to the day after Anderson Brothers withdrew from the transport side of the business, on March 20th 1998, the very last collier sailed from the River Tyne.

TRAMS

Mention should be made of the tram system which operated from the Central Station to the Wingrove Road junction on Fenham Hall Drive. Newcastle Corporation arranged for bus services to link-up for passengers to Westerhope. This was in September 1907. However, after many years of arguments and consultation, the service was extended to Ellesmere Avenue in May 1925. To many locals, the stop is still known as the tram terminus. The service ended in early 1939.

Left: A Newcastle Corporation tram passing Fenham Barracks. Where would the child come from as there were no houses nearby?

ARMSTRONG'S

Over the years, many thousands of 'Geordies' have been conveyed to destinations all over Great Britain in Armstrong Group vehicles.

The Group comprised the parent company R. Armstrong Ltd, Galleys Coaches Ltd and Moordale Bus Services Ltd, and owned a total fleet of fifty buses and coaches.

Each company had retained its own distinctive livery, Armstrong's – green and cream, Galley's – blue and black and Moordale's – red, blue and white.

The Group head office was in Newgate Street opposite the Co-op, whereas Moordale's had an office in nearby Bigg Market and Galley's had a booking office in the east end of the city just off Shields Road. Both Armstrong's and Galley's vehicles were garaged at Westerhope, but Moordale's were kept at their original premises at South Gosforth.

The history of the parent company dated back to 1930, when the late Robert Armstrong began operating miners' contract services in the Westerhope area to the north west of the city.

Private hire work was eventually undertaken and by 1939 some fourteen buses and coaches were in service.

A new depot was opened in Westerhope in 1939 adjoining that owned by Bells Services Ltd, which at that time operated services in the surrounding district. The depot was eventually extended to accommodate 34 vehicles under cover.

During the war years, when private work was limited, buses were employed on contract to RAF airfields under construction at Tranwell and Ouston and when Ouston became operational, a service was introduced from the airfield to Marlborough Crescent bus station via Heddon on the Wall.

Bell's Garage – A group of some of the Armstrong staff outside of their Westerhope Garage acquired from Bell's Services Ltd. Third from left is Robert Armstrong. Also included is Tony Brown, driver and conductor, is holding the timetable. On the far right is William Armstrong.

Armstrong's of Westerhope in the 1960s – Bus Stop outside Runnymede public house.

In August 1954, Armstrong's acquired the 'country' services of Bells Services Ltd.

A daily service was provided between Newcastle and Matfen via Westerhope, Dalton and Stamfordham, the route being extended in a loop to Ryal, Ingoe, Kirkheaton and Waldridge on Saturdays and to Ingoe on Sundays.

One of the oldest established operators on Tyneside – Galley's Motors Ltd, came under Armstrong's control in 1960. Galleys had become a limited company in 1950 having opened a coach booking office at the Haymarket bus station, the office being used as a parcel and enquiry office by all independent operators working into the Haymarket Station.

On the takeover by the Armstrong Group, the company was registered as Galleys Coaches Ltd, concentrating exclusively on excursions, tours and private hire work.

Moordale Bus Service Ltd, a relatively new company, was formed in 1947 but came under the control of Armstrong's in June 1964. Private hire

Westerhope Garage – Robert Armstrong and Jackie Milburn, Newcastle United and England footballer.

and contract work had been undertaken from their Newcastle office and they were the first operator to introduce continental tours from Tyneside. They also had agencies for holiday camps and other British and continental tours.

A typical outing in Armstrong's 1974 Tours Brochure to Scarborough via Stockton, Guisboro', Whitby, Pickering, Helmsley and Stokesley, cost 85p on weekdays and Sundays.

Armstrong's of Westerhope – Mr Eddie Dunn, Managing Director, in 1964.

After having built up such a successful business it was unfortunate that Robert Armstrong died in 1966 at the early age of 58.

The business was then carried on by his nephew Eddie Dunn who had been General Manager of the Group since 1957 and a director since 1963. He became Managing Director in 1964. His cousin Robert Armstrong became a director of the Group.

The maintenance of the Moordale vehicles based at South Gosforth was carried out at the Westerhope depot under the supervision of the local Bobby Wilson, the Chief Engineer.

One of the vehicles was specially equipped for use by Newcastle United Football Club. Eddie had been a Director of the Club from 1981 to 1989.

All the vehicles were always in immaculate condition and were a credit to the managerial, maintenance and driving staff.

In 1989 the Group ceased to function and the business was purchased by the company entitled Proud and Mutual.

THE WESTERHOPE BUS

Local historian, Joe Allison, recalls the days of the Westerhope Bus:

The very first means of transport serving Westerhope, was the old horse drawn brake, which ran between Whorlton Church and Nelson Street, Newcastle. Quite a few local farmers used their own transport of pony and trap. Two of our local haulage families, Hewitson and Anderson, owned and ran brakes in this very competitive means of transport into town. The brake would hold 20 passengers, with the driver perched up on high, to enable him to look back over the passengers heads and, of course, to keep an eye on his rivals, but he was very exposed to the elements. Many tricks were played to get extra customers.

There were two obstacles en route between Westerhope and Newcastle. Going into town was Heathery Shank Bank before you got to Cowgate and then, coming back between Slatyford and Black Swine Farm was Black Bank, which was quite a pull up.

Most of the drivers would set their horses at a gallop to get up these banks, but often failed. The most exciting time was a late Saturday night, when they had a few drunks on board. The most unscrupulous driver would ask his passengers to alight, with the idea of picking them up at the top of the bank again. But he would then smartly turn his horses around, nip back to Newcastle for another load, leaving his passengers stranded on Black Bank just outside Westerhope, but a mile or two from North Walbottle and Callerton.

We have photographs of a private bus that ran through Westerhope to Newcastle in 1906 by a partnership named Locke and Payne, but the first regular Corporation motor bus service started in 1912 – running from Fenham Barracks, or the corner of Hunter's Road, through Westerhope to Whorlton Church.

One of the first drivers was Abie Hunnam, who eventually married a Westerhope girl, Mary Hannah, daughter of James Bainbridge of Bainbridge Buildings. The village people were riding on a motor bus for the first time and Abie became very popular as the steady driver, and he certainly had to be with his double decker Tilling Stevens engine, solid tyres and the pot-holed

"DOLLAR PRINCESS."

MOTOR CHAR-A-BANC TOURS.

DARLINGTON
Royal Show.

JUNE 28th — JULY 3rd, 1920.

The Leyland Chara-de-Luxe "DOLLAR PRINCESS" will leave
CENTRAL STATION at 8 a.m. daily.
Leave DARLINGTON at 6.30 p.m.

Return Fare:—
MONDAY and TUESDAY **15/-**
Other Days **12/6**

Tickets may be had on application to:—
THE NEWBURN CHAR-A-BANC
AND HAULAGE CO., Ltd.,
Newburn-on-Tyne.
'Phone—Lemington 59.

The "Dollar Princess" poster from 1920.

The "Dollar Princess" Westerhope in 1920, This type of charabanc catered for outings throughout the North East. A typical tour from Newcastle to the Royal Show at Darlington in 1920 – Cost 12/6d (62p) return.

state of the road. The driver had very little protection from the weather, and both the stairway and top deck, which youngsters enjoyed, were open.

From a newspaper cutting dated 1912, it quotes "A timetable has been arranged for the running of the buses. The fares vary. No fare being less than 1d. Children under three allowed free and under 12s, half price. A charge will be made for luggage. The buses will not stop on heavy gradients and workmen coming from work will only be allowed to use the top deck." This meant the miners of course. I remember a 3d single fare to Newcastle and a 4d return, from the bottom of Beaumont Terrace. What a rough ride from Whorlton to the Barracks.

In view of the bus service starting, the Corporation had lifted the level of Black Bank, which made it easier for the heavy double-decker. Then at Slatyford, a ford (giving Slatyford its name) ran across the main road, and could be very tricky to cross in winter. Next came the formidable task of climbing Heathery Shank Bank, the Corporation didn't do much with that gradient until much later. The Heathery Shank was a longer, but steadier gradient, in contrast to Black Bank, which had been shorter but steeper.

Driver Abe Hunnam stands outside his Tillings Steven 34 – seat double decker 1916 at the Whorlton terminus of Newcastle Corporation's first motor bus service. It started on May 12th 1912, and ran through Westerhope from Fenham Barracks. A notice warned "That these buses will not stop on heavy gradients and workmen returning from work will only be allowed to ride on outside."

I remember many times as a schoolboy on a busy Saturday, with my father, the full bus sticking half-way up Heathery Shank, and the people on the top deck being asked to get off and walk to the top. I recall an incident on the same bank, and which the older residents of the village still talk about. Tom Bainbridge (son of James) was driving a full Corporation bus up the bank, when his engine failed, but Tom very coolly stuck to the wheel and steered it safely back to the bottom. During the First World War, the Corporation, owing to the shortage of petrol, had to resort to gas to power their buses, and we lost our enjoyable top deck temporarily, by the presence of a gas bag on top. The Corporation buses were blue and the Westerhope service number was 3.

Obviously, there have been tremendous changes in public transport from those early days.

The bus passes the Jingling Gate public house.

IT STARTED IN WEST AVENUE
BY JOAN COCKBURN (née WAKE)

I was born on the 18th August 1940 at 134 West Avenue. My dad was an electrical engineer who worked initially for a company called Barker's in Gateshead, but eventually had his own business. My mam was Annie nee Lenaghan, a well known Westerhope family. She had several jobs – she was employed at Dillon's nursery (where Cowell's is now) and gathered the roses there for marketing. She worked at the News Theatre in Newcastle where she met Gene Autry the famous movie cowboy. She was also an usherette at the Picture Palace (The Orion). Her final job was at the Newcastle University.

The Lenaghan side of my family were well known in the village. My grandmother lived in 8 Greenfield Avenue and my uncle John Frances Lenaghan was a Newburn Urban District Councillor and has a plaque in the Westerhope Community Association Building for services to the community. My Aunt Cassie lived at 3 Matlock Gardens, having married a Wing Commander. The house was struck by lightning, the chimney collapsed and a fire occurred.

My only sibling was my sister Theresa and we both attended the Convent of the Sacred Heart in Fenham. I can't recall getting any pocket money but we still bought sweets etc. We provided our own entertainment – hopscotch, marbles, tops and whips and skipping under the gas light, with one end of the rope fastened to the lamp post. We also played pranks such as knocky nine door.

In the winter months we helped our parents with the making of proggy mats on long frames with hessian material stretched between with a selected pattern. We each had a progger tool which penetrated the hessian and then you pulled the clipping material through by a notch in the progger. A clippie mat illustrating the heritage wheel has just been installed at the entrance of the Westerhope Residents Association building (The Tute) on the Hillhead Road.

Joan's Grandfather, James Lenaghan, born in County Mayo, Ireland. He broke his back in a colliery accident and died shortly afterwards.

On West Avenue, known locally as 'Clarty Avenue', we had John Dryden's Farm and his house is still there today. All the neighbourhood collected potato peelings and vegetable matter for swill to feed his pigs and I recall taking orders for his chickens for friends. Families in the early days didn't have washing machines and so they went to Dryden's who had several machines to do their washing. Almost opposite our house was Highfield House, which had been the farm house for the Varty family, but was now occupied by the Lawrenson's. They developed market gardens and they spread the waste products from the abattoir on their land with the result that the village was plagued with bluebottles in the late 1940s.

We loved playing in the nearby fields making daisy chains. We also loved visiting Mrs Stanley's corner shop displaying lovely sweets. My favourites were marzipan teacakes, toffee bars with banana in the middle and Cadbury's Milk Tray chocolate. Around the corner, lived the old lady Mrs. Walker and further along Mrs. Fairless with her lovely garden with its huge Monkey Puzzle tree. Next to our house we had Stan Holdsworth's market garden with his main products – tomatoes, dahlias and chrysanthemums. The tomatoes were outstanding with various types and my dad loved to eat them fried in butter with salt and pepper on them. We always went there for our salads – lettuce, scallions and cucumbers – so fresh you could smell them quite a distance away. Our other purchases were made at Allan's Stores where the off license was and the Co-op.

We loved the walk along Newbiggin Lane to Newbiggin Hall with the nearby bluebell woods and the pond with the ducks. Then back to Runnymede, the house belonging to the Rev William Wakenshaw, with the tennis court at the front and the orchard at the back. He had twin girls. Next to Runnymede was Denton Grove where Mr Foster had his ice cream factory. He lived in Highfield Road. The park was almost opposite our house in West Avenue, it was kept immaculate by George Howarth the greenkeeper. We

Joan's maternal great grandparents – Mr. & Mrs. William Best. They both had been born and lived in Ireland before coming to England.

could always hear the ping of the tennis balls from the many courts. The bowling clubs were very popular. Joe Allison was a regular there and he played for Northumberland County as did Jacky Hancock who also played in the England team.

I left school at fourteen years of age when I had rheumatic fever, then got my first job as an usherette at the Orion. Mr Leslie Longhorn was the manager and Mrs Longhorn sat in the small kiosk in the entrance selling ice cream, sweets and taking bookings for future performances. The stairs to the upper floor were on the opposite side and when patrons got to the top, the usherette would tell them to "Dook" otherwise their silhouette would be projected onto the screen. Cowboy films were very popular and were generally shown on Mondays, Wednesdays, Fridays and Sundays. Children attended the matinees on Saturday mornings – generally paying by getting the deposit back from the lemonade bottles they had collected.

My husband to be worked at Harris's Pilton Gardens. He had lived in an orphanage, then came to Westerhope and lodged with a Mrs. Jones' family in West Avenue. We were married at the registry office. My sister Theresa was my bridesmaid. She was secretary for five doctors in a medical practise. Our bouquets were beautiful and were produced by Sarah Gaskins. David, my husband left Harris's and went to work for British Telecom. He became the supervisor for their 999 system and retired at 60. We had two children, Steven and Judith. David only had three years in retirement before he died at home here at Mangrove Close on St John's Estate. We had forty years of

Joan and her husband David on their wedding day – 3rd November 1966.

happy marriage. I still have my wedding outfit and hat – it certainly wouldn't fit me now, as I have had health problems with cellulitis.

Now we have two grandchildren, David fourteen and Sarah twelve years old – my son Steven's family.

I have had a lovely life here in Westerhope and just love living here and how I enjoyed the "Westerhope Walkabout" booklet.

Mr Lowrison, the market gardener, once said to me: "Be grateful that you knew Westerhope as it was."

WESTERHOPE VILLAGE RESIDENTS' ASSOCIATION

Sheila Graham, a founder member and present Secretary of WVRA, gives this history of the Association:

Westerhope Village Residents' Association was formed in August 1988. It was formed out of frustration, a frustration felt by most residents that the local authority was doing nothing about the general decline in the area. Residents felt Westerhope was fast losing its identity and, being proud of our village, decided to do something about this.

With the help and guidance of Bob Morgan, one of our local councillors, we decided to form a Residents' Association. We set up a steering committee with ten willing volunteers. All like minded people who were interested in the environment in which we lived. We approached local residents by knocking on doors asking them to sign a petition to be sent to the local authority on the state of the roads and footpaths in the village. We also asked if residents' were prepared to make a contribution of 50p per household to get the Association up and running. The support from the local people was phenomenal; we had chosen an issue on roads and pathways that all residents were concerned about. The petition went off to the local authority and of course the answer, as always came down to having no money, adding, Westerhope was not on a priority list for this type of improvement. To cut a very long story short, with the help of our local councillors we stood our ground and, within five years of presenting the petition to the local authority, all the side roads and pavements within the village had been upgraded.

Sheila Graham receiving an award on behalf of Westerhope Village Residents' Association in 2007 from Newcastle City Council for their work in the community. From left to right: Maureen Smith, Stan Potter, Audrey Maddocks, Mary Embleton, Sheila Graham, Vic Bond, Anne Trotter, Linda Cumming, Dorothy Toward, Maureen Graham.

During this time, we met Bill Lamb who worked for the local authority in Recreation and Leisure. Bill encouraged us to get involved in the concept of 'Britain in Bloom'. He explained the procedure but stressed it would be very hard work. However, we decided we needed to show the local authority that we were serious about improving our village and that we, as residents, were prepared to contribute to this end.

We started with 10 large wooden barrels strategically placed (with permission from the Highways Department) and invited local school children to help us plant them. Our committee and various sub committees met on a regular basis to discuss and plan our way forward, with ideas and suggestions from the local community. As we could afford it, we introduced more flower tubs. We have spent many cold nights in a garage, potting on plants to fill the tubs. When it got to the point of needing over 7000 plants, we were offered the facilities for potting on at Jesmond Dene Nurseries, this was advantageous because of the volume of plants. Now, however we raise the funds, usually through our annual summer fair and grand summer raffle and pay the local authority to plant the multitude of pots and tubs we have acquired over the years. We, as a committee, do help out with weeding planting and tidying as and when we can.

We now have numerous flower beds, additional planters, trees and seating areas throughout the village. We have won numerous awards for our efforts, although the gold medal has always eluded us!

In 1991, we celebrated the village centenary. In August that year, we held our main event which included a parade through the village, both motorcade and walkers, to the Miners' Institute on Hillheads Road. Researching this year took a long time as we had so many activities arranged and so I have created a full section on the Westerhope Village Centenary Celebrations (on page 59).

We tried for the next couple of years to maintain the momentum of offering regular outings and activities for the residents. We were very lucky to have Vic Bond, a local bus driver, on our committee and Vic organised the hire of 'The Green Machine' (a rather special single decker bus) which took us to visit Sunderland Illuminations. This outing proved so popular, we had to visit at least twice, once for adults only and then a trip to include children. We organised a trip to the seaside – South Shields - for children. We did an evening mystery tour – which ended up in Bellingham, where supper was provided in two local pubs. Add to this, car boot sales, coffee mornings, music from the Chapel House Middle School Steel Band, a Beau and Belles evening of sing-a-long nostalgic music, the Newcastle Male Voice Chorus a night of choral singing by the Ravenswood Singers – all very much supported and appreciated by local people. Sadly because of work commitments, we as a committee, found all this extra

A regular scene as Stan Potter and Audrey Maddocks sell the annual summer raffle tickets outside the village post office.

voluntary work exhausting and had to curtail the activities.

In 1995, we redesigned one of our small flower beds with Peace Roses to mark VE day. The engraved plaque was unveiled by the then Lord Mayor Councillor Bob Brown. Later that year, we introduced a raised flower bed on Stamfordham Road and again we had the ground consecrated by Wes Blakey, the local minister, had a plaque erected and, to this day, this garden is used as our official Remembrance Garden, where every November we place our wreath on behalf of the village residents' in memory of the armed forces who, throughout the years, have paid the ultimate sacrifice.

As the new millennium approached, we decided to raise funds to have a permanent symbol of our community commitment. It all really started with a telephone call from the Reverend Wes Blakey from the Methodist Church who asked what the Residents' Association were planning to do to celebrate the new millennium and could the church and residents maybe come together and make the year 2000 special. A small committee of seven was formed. The idea of a clock as the main project for the year was decided because of the history of the clock tower on the original Methodist Church. This had been demolished during the 1970s to make way for the church as we know it today. Many years after the old church was gone, people looked up to where the clock had been; it was fair to say the old clock had been sadly missed.

The Residents' Association took the idea of a new clock to their AGM in 1999 and a plan was formulated, although at this stage the design of the clock was not! Local residents were given the opportunity to vote on their choice of design for the clock and most went for a less ornate design and something in keeping with the surroundings in which it was to be introduced.

Fund raising started with an approach to local businesses, donations were made and we were on our way! An application to the 'Awards for All' lottery fund was made, but community activity continued. At Christmas time, the idea of 'Light a Light' on the village Christmas tree was organised and very well supported, raising over £1000. A charity night was organised by Westerhope Excelsior Social Club and raised £1600 – by this time there was no turning back! From sponsored slims to soft toy sales, choirs singing and small brown donation envelopes, our funds expanded. Having our grant application turned down was the most disappointing aspect of the whole project;

however we had to get the adrenaline flowing once more and go out and find more sponsorship. Eventually through the generosity of Bass Brewery, we were back on our target of £10,000 and the installation of the clock was imminent.

The unveiling of the clock took place on the 10th June 2000. The Reverend Wes Blakey thanked the community for all their efforts and the honour of unveiling a commemorative plaque was undertaken by local resident and historian Joe Allison along with his wife Dorothy. I think it is fair to say the clock is now a main feature on Stamfordham Road. Westerhope Village Residents' Association were unique in being the only city voluntary

Committee members check the time against the new Millennium Clock.

organisation that celebrated the millennium with a permanent memorial – our village clock.

The clock maker was William Potts and Sons of Leeds, and the ground and ancillary work was carried out by G. Bowman, a local builder.

A time capsule was also buried in the ground next to the clock. This contains local memorabilia, centenary china and photographs, along with contributions from local schools. It must remain underground until 2030! There is a certificate in the Methodist Church safe declaring this – and we as a Residents' Association also have a copy of the certificate.

We have reduced our fund raising to one main event per year, as we feel we cannot be continually going to the local people and businesses within the community for funds. Our main fund raising event is our annual summer fair – this is hard work, and let me say very much weather dependant! The event is always very well supported by the local community. We hold a grand raffle each year when most of the businesses in the village contribute a prize. This raffle is drawn at the annual summer fair, which is usually held on the first Saturday of August and although we have visited different venues throughout the Westerhope Ward, the 'home' of the fair is now the Methodist Church hall and grounds. We continue to have a very good working relationship with the members of this church and the position of the church in the centre of the village is vital to community involvement and participation. All the funds raised by the Residents' Association go back into the village by the way of flowers, tubs, planters seats etc. Every flower planted in Westerhope village is a symbol of community support. We have also, for many years now, erected a Christmas tree with lights in the grounds of the church and the community are encouraged to sing carols around the tree just before Christmas each year.

During the interim years, we worked tirelessly for our community, introducing more flowers, trees, seats to make our village a special place to live. However, although the beautification of the village is essential, so is our support or objection to various changes being made around us. Parking on pavements has always (and still is) a big safety issue for pedestrians and so the Local Authority decided to erect barriers to create safe walking areas – this turned out to be a somewhat controversial decision. Differences of opinion arose among residents regarding the two supermarkets in the village – although we fought the democratic corner, we have had to learn to live with changes. We lost the local authority run care home Pilton House (on the corner of Newbiggin Lane and Stamfordham Road) but gained new housing on that site and a new private care home on Wheatfield Road. We lost the local police station and gained a private children's nursery.

The Village Clock was funded and erected by the local community to commemorate the Millennium – unveiled by Mr & Mrs Joe Allison on 10th June 2000.

The environment around us continued to change, with the most controversial being the Boundary Committee for England deciding in 2004 to go ahead and split our village. Basically, north of Stamfordham Road was to be included in the Woolsington Ward of Newcastle City Council and south of Stamfordham Road was to stay in Westerhope Ward. We wrote numerous letters protesting, however the Electoral Commission accepted the proposals to divide the village, with no modification to the plans. Westerhope Baby Clinic at the corner of Highfield Road and Stamfordham Road having long since gone has been replaced by a Wellness Centre. The Examination Board building on Stamfordham Road and Wheatfield Road has been demolished by new owners Lidl, however the land is once again up for sale, possibly for an affordable housing development. The land on which the British Bakeries (one of the most important employers of local people) is for sale, again, as a possible housing development. We have learnt to live with these changes, and carry on for the good of our community.

As our 20th birthday was approaching, we decided we needed to celebrate this momentous occasion. We talked of a community party but then came upon the idea of a lasting monument. After discussions with the local history society and the local councillors, we thought the idea of bringing an old mining pulley wheel into the village, as a reminder of the mining heritage that was so important to the foundation of our village.

The Village Clock to commemorate the Millennium.

George Graham, local NUM secretary and community worker, knew of a redundant pulley wheel in the grounds of Stakeford (Northumberland) Council yard. Local councillors, officials and Residents' Association members went to investigate. This was in October 2007. We were encouraged and persuaded to take two half wheels. The wheel was from Ellington Colliery, the last working deep mine in Northumberland. Had we not located and retrieved the wheel it would have been scrapped and lost forever, along with the history and heritage surrounding it.

The newly refurbished wheel was to be sited on the roundabout adjacent to the A1, on the main trunk road west of Newcastle – at the entrance to Westerhope village and on West Denton Way. Because of this prominent position of the roundabout, it would be visible to thousands of people on a daily basis – motorists, people using public transport and pedestrians. The main funding for the wheel was provided by fund raising efforts and contributions from Westerhope, Denton and Woolsington Wards.

The wheel was duly transported to the Jesmond Dene nurseries where it was to be sand blasted and repainted. The timetable for the project progressed in earnest and planning consent was granted on the 14th April 2008. The decorative name Westerhope was started. May and June saw the site being cleared and prepared, the structural foundations for the wheel laid and the erection of the feature plinth begun. Running alongside these activities was the lighting installation. July saw the base of the wheel in place followed shortly afterwards by the top of the wheel being added. The tidying of the site began and the name plate was added along with a coal like substance around the base. This led us up to the initiation ceremony on Saturday 2nd August 2008. The Wansbeck Ashington Miners' brass band started the proceedings, by playing the miners' hymn 'Gresford' followed by Ian Lavery the President of the National Union of Mineworkers presenting the wheel to the community. The Lord Mayor and Lady Mayoress of Newcastle attended along with local historians, village residents' and retired miners. It was a simple but moving ceremony. An amazing achievement – within one year our dream had become a reality, this was made possible by the sheer determination of local councillors Marc Donnelly, Pat Hillicks and Neil Hamilton, Local Authority officials, Tom Peacock of the Local History Society, George Graham

Residents Association Committee members look on as the Millennium time capsule is being buried.

local NUM official, Alan Stewart NUM Secretary from Ellington, Ian Lavery National President of the NUM and of course the Westerhope Village Residents' Association.

Running along side the wheel project it was decided to have a Heritage Festival. The Westerhope Community Centre – formerly the Miners' Institute – was having a grand refurbishment and the re-opening date coincided with the initiation of the wheel. So 'Our Heritage Festival' was planned. The Westerhope Community Partnership co-ordinated the event, with different groups taking on different tasks. The Westerhope Village Residents Association decided to hold our annual summer fair on this day. The Lord Mayor of Newcastle Councillor David Wood opened the proceedings. We had a fantastic day of community activity – even the pouring rain couldn't spoil the fun. Two 'old' buses were driven by volunteers on a circular route around the local area to pick up and drop off people attending the festival. This proved to be a wonderful and well used part of the proceedings. There was brass bands, singing and dancing, craft stalls, rides for the children, hoopla, quoits, rolling coins, football, the fire service and local police – there was literally something for everyone. Local schools were invited to join in with organised art projects with the festival banner in pride of place. The community proggy mat (everyone was encouraged to have a go), is on permanent display at Westerhope Community Centre. We even had special dispensation to bring the North Walbottle Pit Banner out of Woodhorn Colliery Museum for the afternoon. It was just a fantastic day – very hard work to organise but the reward was seeing all the support from local people on an afternoon when the rain poured down.

The Westerhope Proggy Mat – designed by the Rev. Anne Marr.

Even as I write this short history of our Village Residents' Association, we are preparing for this year's annual summer fair – everything will be in place on time, even the sun we hope! Vic Bond, Chair of the Association will keep us all – Anne Trotter, Audrey Maddocks, Dorothy Toward, Linda Cumming, Mary Embleton, Maureen Graham, Maureen Smith, Stan Potter and myself Sheila Graham focused and on target for yet another successful year. Long may they continue. It has been a pleasure (well most of the time) and privilege to work for Westerhope Village. Without the splendid support of local business and local residents, this Association could not function, and we certainly realise we could not carry out the assignments set us.

CENTENARY CELEBRATIONS

When Westerhope Village Residents' Association was formed in 1988, the committee were unaware that the village was due to celebrate 100 years of existence only three years later in 1991. We were made aware of this fact by the local History Society and decided to try to make 1991 special. The Association did lots of promotions and fundraising and, with the support of the local community, made the Westerhope Centenary Celebrations something that should be recorded in the varied history of Westerhope Village.

We had heard many times of the historical transition from Westerhope Garden Village to that of Westerhope Pit Village and so, as a committee, wanted everyone to know how proud we were of our mining connections. It was decided to try to locate two old pit tubs, have them renovated, plant them up with flowers and place them at each end of our village. To get redundant pit tubs seemed like an easy task, as pits were closing, or had closed all around us. However, after many phone calls and visits to various pit heads, George and Sheila Graham located tubs at Iveson Coal Company in County Durham. The owner agreed we could have two tubs free of charge when it was explained what we wanted to do with them. A bottle of whisky was given in gratitude and the two chosen tubs were transported by local business man Andy Curry, to a unit in Kingston Park where they were restored – again, because there was no charge – a bottle of whisky exchanged hands! We had brass plaques inscribed and mounted on the tubs, placed the tubs on authentic rail track and they have adorned our village ever since with beautiful floral displays.

We wanted to make a great effort in bringing back the community spirit of Westerhope and so it was decided to have months of non stop activities, leading up to the main event of a procession through the village, followed by a carnival. Our first attempt at bringing the community together was an Old Time Music Hall entertainment group. This event was held in the Excelsior Social Club and around 350 people attended and it was a great success.

The Carnival committee float.

As always, a very popular event – organised by the local History Society – was held over a period of 5 days commencing on Tuesday 11th June and followed through to Saturday 15th June. The event included a comprehensive display of old photographs and memorabilia and was displayed in the Methodist Church hall throughout each day, and then each evening a slide show was shown. To end a fantastically well supported week, a walk through the village was arranged on Saturday 15th June to point out places of historic interest. This event was again extremely well attended and generated a great deal of interest and enthusiasm from local people.

To coincide with the above event, the Residents' Association and the Methodist Church organised a Flower Festival to take place on Saturday 15th and Sunday 16th June. The displays were donated by various businesses and organisations from the village. The ladies from the church provided refreshments on both days. The week ended with lots of exhausted volunteers, but because of the great success of the celebrations, local people were asking what's next!

On the 22nd June, we organised our very own Antiques Road Show, again held in the Methodist Church hall. We had local experts living in the village that offered their time and experience and came along to realistically value family heirlooms. As per the real television show, there was a mixture of smiling and disillusioned faces!

On the 25th June, it was the turn of Westerhope First School. The school held an open day when all the children and staff were encouraged to dress in costume. Games from a previous era were played, old school photographs were on display and the general public were invited to step back in time during the school day.

Millennium Celebrations.

We had a well earned rest of two weeks before our next organised event on the 10th

July, which was staged by the Westerhope War Games Group. The re-enactment chosen was that of the Battle of Tokar from 1891. This war took place on the Red Sea coast between dervish forces of the Khalifa and the British and Egyptian Armies. The group used 25 mm metal figures – made and painted by themselves – realistic terrain, buildings etc. The game was fast flowing and the group welcomed participation from any interested spectators – young and not so young. The aim of the war game was not to glorify or diminish war and conflict, but to stimulate the logistics, difficulties, hopelessness and futility of armed conflict. It was fun and as the name implies – it was a game.

On the 13th July, we welcomed a church full of local residents' to an evening of entertainment with the Ravenswood Singers, a very talented choir of 70 or so singers – who gave a wonderful production of songs from stage shows and films.

On the 27th July, Mr and Mrs Herford, of 409 Stamfordham Road, invited everyone to a Centenary garden party. The weather was kind, even if a bit windy, but, like all other events organised, was well supported and we even made a little money from a variety of stalls.

We had a break of around three weeks before the main event of the year. That is not to say we were resting! Believe me, it took many hours of arranging and re arranging but, in all my time as a Westerhope resident, I have never been more proud of my contribution to the local community than I was on the 17th August 1991. Well, we planned and arranged everything, down to the last detail, however, something we had no control over was the weather.

We woke to a rather miserable cloudy morning and all the action began around 7 am when the marquee was

Newcastle Brewery's dray horses lead the parade through the village and on to the Institute field.

being erected on the Institute field. The motorcade and parade through the village was due to start at 11 am, but prior to this time we, as a committee, still had lots to do – erecting our own tent, arranging the layout of the festival field, just generally making sure that things were organised and ready for the hundreds of people we expected to attend. The local police had supported our efforts, but had instructed us that the motorcade only could leave from the Redewood School site on Wellfield Lane, the most easterly site suitable. The walkers needed to join the parade half way through the village and so congregated in Westerhope Excelsior Social Club car park and then intermingled with the motorcade from the bottom of Wheatfield Road. The procession took us along Stamfordham Road, up Beaumont Terrace, right onto West Avenue, continuing onto Langdon Road, left onto Downend Road, then right onto Hillhead Road and finally onto the Institute field, where the carnival was to be held. It was awesome to see the planning and preparation come into place. The parade was led by the dray horses from Scottish and Newcastle Breweries, followed by an open topped bus provided by Busways. A local resident with a horse drawn gypsy caravan followed. The Residents' Association float followed the 'Old Rington's Tea' bus. Then came the Guides and Brownies, marching to the music from the Backworth Colliery Band. Vintage cars took their place followed by the Postman Pat (a great favourite with the children) truck.

Warburton's Bakers vintage vehicle with local children were next and then the Boys' Brigade, Scouts and Beavers followed. Anderson's, an established haulage company of many years from the village, provided an old haulage truck and this was followed by the Westerhope Excelsior Social Club staff float – all dressed in costumes of one hundred years ago. A motor float of local musicians playing their individual instruments were followed by a vintage fire engine. The Westerhope Labour party became involved in the march next, with traditional costume and placards reading 'Votes for Women'. Silksworth Colliery Band followed closely by the North Walbottle pit banner and retired miners took pride of place – this sight brought many lumps to many throats! Callerton Kids on their float were followed by a regular army truck with a police vehicle following up at the rear.

As you can imagine, this parade took a good hour to travel through the village onto the carnival field, but the atmosphere that went along with it was joyful, even ecstatic.

The Lord Mayor of Newcastle upon Tyne, Councillor Tom Marr, opened the festival at around 1 o'clock and then the activities within the marquee and the arenas began. We had organised a fancy dress parade, five a side football tournament, a bowls tournament, tug of war, Punch and Judy shows along with roundabouts and shuggy boats for the children. Displays from the Territorial Army, Health Bus, British Red Cross, Save the Children, Blood Transfusion Service, Police Crime Prevention and St John's Ambulance Brigade were scattered around the festival field. The marquee was full of craft stalls, which included local ladies making lace, proggy mat making, fabric painting, hand made ornaments and dried flower arrangements. The local nursing home, Pilton House, ran a tombola, centenary china was on sale, ironmongery and graphic designs were on display. Local churches were involved, the Westerhope and Whorlton WI made and displayed home made cakes. Westerhope Training Unit on Newbiggin Lane brought along items made in the unit and of course everyone's favourite the Local History Group had a wonderful display of local memorabilia. There was literally something for everyone – and still the rain only threatened!

To say we were supported would be an understatement. People came literally from miles around – the

Michelle Musgrave thanks the Lord Mayor, Cllr Tom Marr, and his wife the Lady Mayoress for their contribution.

vintage bus provided by Busways and driven by our now chairman Vic Bond (in full costume I might add) transported people from local areas, but people came of their own accord from a far greater distance – oh! and I must not forget we had the blessing of her Majesty the Queen in the form of a letter congratulating Westerhope on its centenary.

We received many, many, complimentary comments, both on the day – and later. Everyone had enjoyed a wonderful celebration, but just as things were beginning to quieten down – around 4 pm – the heavens opened and the rain that fell was torrential. Really the weather – which is always in charge of these outdoor events – brought the curtain down on one of the most memorable days in the history of Westerhope Village.

OUR HERITAGE WHEEL

For several years, discussions have taken place as to how to commemorate the history of North Walbottle Colliery. The Village Residents' Association and the Local History Society came to the conclusion that if we could acquire a mining wheel, it could be displayed at the entrance to Westerhope, with a suitable plaque giving brief details of the village and the mine. We were successful in acquiring a suitable wheel from Ellington Colliery, the last deep mine to close in the North East area.

The wheel was completely refurbished and mounted on a stone plinth with WESTERHOPE emblazoned on the top half.

It was unveiled on 2nd August 2008 in the presence of the Lord Mayor of Newcastle – Cllr David Wood, Ian Lavery, the President of the National Union of Mineworkers Association, Sheila Graham of the Westerhope Residents' Association, Marc Donnelly – Ward Councillor, George Graham who had been responsible for acquiring the wheel, and Tom Peacock, the Chairman of the Local History Society.

It was a splendid and memorable occasion with the display of the North Walbottle Colliery banner from Woodhorn Colliery Museum and with the support of the Ashington Colliery Brass Band and a huge public presence.

Following the unveiling ceremony, we all proceeded to the recently refurbished Community Association Centre, (formerly the Miners' Institute) for the official opening by the Lord Mayor and in the afternoon, our Heritage Festival continued in the form of a family picnic with everyone invited to wear period outfits.

In spite of the dreadful weather, the day had great public support and

The opening of the Heritage Wheel. Left to right: Tom Peacock, Councillor Marc Donnelly, George Graham, Ian Lavery, Lord Mayor of Newcastle Councillor David Wood, Councillor Margaret Wood, the Mayoress and Sheila Graham.

the event culminated with the release of 250 blue and pink balloons.

During the lead up to the Heritage Festival and on the day, all the groups in the ward had contributed, particularly the 'umbrella group' the Westerhope Community Partnership. The local schools were also involved. With the help of the Ward Committee and officers from the council, each of the three primary schools produced their own 'banner' which the schools kept. A fourth banner was produced by the young people from all three schools and this fourth banner is usually displayed on the wall of the Westerhope Community Association.

Another lasting memento of the event is a proggy mat, which was produced on the day. Rev Anne Marr was responsible for the design in advance, and anyone who wished to 'do a bit' was able to do so during the Festival. Anne then completed the proggy mat and it has since been framed and hung in the entrance area of the Westerhope Community Association. The event was widely publicised in the various local newspapers and was supported by the BBC, appearing in their *Look North* programme on the same evening. It was an occasion which will long be remembered by the residents of Westerhope and others in neighbouring Wards and a fitting and lasting tribute to both the village of Westerhope and the colliery at North Walbottle.

IRIS SMITH, MBE

The history of my family's life in Westerhope dates back to 1904 when my maternal grandparents John and Sarah Darling moved from Gateshead to Beaumont Terrace with their four daughters. John had been a butcher all his working life, working in large houses including Alnwick Castle. He had now been appointed as the first caretaker at Westerhope School, but had to wait to live in the house being built for the caretaker alongside the school. My mother Mildred was only four years old but had to walk to the 'Tin School' on Wheatfield Road as there was no provision for infants at the new school. The first Headmaster at the school was Mr Herdman.

Meanwhile, my father's parents, Walter and Hannah Smith, had moved from Burnopfield to Blucher with their son and four daughters. Walter was a Blacksmith.

John William (Bill) was six years old when they came to Blucher and attended Walbottle School until he was thirteen. His father was determined that Bill would not follow in his footsteps, so he obtained an apprenticeship for boot and shoe making. At seventeen he joined the army in the First World War, seeing active service in France and Germany and was in the Victory March through Germany.

When Bill returned home, he used to walk from Blucher, up past Arthur's Farm and down Hillhead Road. It was during these walks that he met Mildred. Their courtship began, but Mildred would not marry while her mother needed her. Sarah died in 1923, so Bill and Mildred married on the 1st January 1925 at 8 am in Newburn Parish Church. They made their home in the School House until 1926, helping John Darling to look after the school and the grounds.

In 1926, the family moved to Stamfordham Road and Bill, with the help of his father, cleared ground next to Kendal Green East and erected a hut where Bill started a boot and shoe repair business. The business flourished and Bill eventually erected a brick building to replace the timber hut.

Bill was a popular personality in the village, but due to ill health, retired in 1961. Mildred died in 1974 and Bill in 1987.

In 1927, they had moved to 9 Windsor

Westerhope Council School's first caretaker – John William Darling and daughter Mildred Grace Darling (Mrs Smith – Iris' mother).

Crescent. Their first of three daughters, Violet, was born on the 23rd October 1925 at the School House. Their second daughter Olive in 1928 and their third, Iris, in 1935.

They were all christened and confirmed at St John's Church (Whorlton) and are regular worshippers there.

I was the third of the Smith sisters to attend Westerhope School, Violet in 1930, Olive in 1933 and I joined them in 1940.

I still remember all of the teachers at the school – Mr Reed was the Headmaster, then Mr Laidler, Mr Shevills, Miss Baxter, Miss Nairn, Miss Wilkinson and Miss Bean who was the first teacher in the Infant Department.

One of the highlights at school was when the 'Bird Man' came. We all assembled in the hall when this man came who was excellent at imitating birds. He thrilled all of us. When walking home from school we often saw the cows coming up Newbiggin Lane to North Avenue to get milked. We also saw the Italian prisoners of war at

Harris's gardens peering over the fence to whistle to the ladies as they passed.

We had evacuees from London at the school. They found a big difference in living in a country village, but they joined in all of our activities. In 1941 there was a very heavy snowstorm, the snow being so high that we were walking along the hedges of the fields to get to school. Another war time memory was taking a jam jar and having it filled with drinking chocolate which had been sent from America. At the end of the war we all received certificate cards and a two shilling coin.

A particularly unpleasant memory was having to use the toilets at the rear of the school yard. They were buckets covered with wooden seats. A sluice van came once a week to empty them and you could sometimes see the contents dripping over the yard!

My friends at school, all still living in Westerhope, were Sheila Handley, Audrey Thompson, Kathleen Stokoe, Jean Hepple and Mary Clark. We all enjoyed the usual childhood games – skipping, hopscotch, tops and whips, tiggy, mount a cuddy and the mischievous games like knocky nine doors.

I also attended Sunday School at St John's Church with the leader, Rev. Johnstone and my sister Violet was one of my teachers. I recall meeting a christening party coming to Church and being given the customary gifts of a parcel with a piece of coal, a candle, a scone and a sixpenny piece. It was Jim Blight's christening.

I left school at 15 and went to Underwoods to take a secretarial course. I then joined Smith's the Printers in Newcastle, becoming secretary before starting my own printing business for eight years.

I then became an administrator for the Northumberland Branch of the Red Cross Society and retired at 60 years of age.

My hobbies had been cycling, reading, the Girls' Guild and a member of the Anglican Young People's Association – AYPA, plus holidays.

Childhood holidays were spent at Newton by the Sea. We self-catered, taking with us Harris's tomatoes, ham from the Co-op and the family fruit cake.

Later we went to Canada, the USA and countries in Europe.

My sister Violet and I enjoy caravanning. We have a caravan at Warren Mill near Bamburgh and we often stay there for several days.

A special event occurred in 1995 when I was awarded the MBE in the New Year's Honours Lists for 50 years of voluntary service in the Red Cross Society. I received it at Buckingham Palace from Prince Charles.

Miss Iris Smith MBE, Buckingham Palace, 21st May 1996.

WHORLTON AND WESTERHOPE WOMEN'S INSTITUTE

The first meeting of Whorlton & Westerhope Women's Institute was held in June 1930 in St John's Church Hall, Whorlton, the membership being made up of ladies from the three mining villages of North Walbottle, Callerton and the largest, Westerhope. These villages were all in the Parish of Whorlton, hence the name 'Whorlton & Westerhope'. Appropriately the first President was Mrs McGee, wife of the manager of North Walbottle Colliery.

Membership in that first year numbered 76 (annual fee 2 shillings) but the meetings proved so popular that, by 1935-36, we had moved to the larger hall in the new 'Miners Welfare' (now Westerhope Community Association) on Hillhead Road, where we still meet. We were at that time, in Northumberland Federation and were in the 'Hadrian Group' along with Newton, Wylam, Heddon-on-the-Wall, Throckley and Blucher & Walbottle.

1940 saw the Institute ladies 'doing their bit' for the War effort and our records show that 422 pairs of socks were knitted and sent to men of the three armed services, together with an equal number of scarves and helmets. Each Christmas from 1940-45 gifts to the value of 7/6d (37.5p) were sent to British prisoners of war. The fund was finally wound up in 1947 and cash gifts were made to 85 returning servicemen and women.

Institute logo.

The membership was now approaching 200 and, such was the demand, that it became necessary to introduce a waiting list. From such a large membership, a strong choir was formed in 1934 and from then until the beginning of the war, they took part in the many Northumberland Federation Choral Competitions, winning First Place on four occasions. After the war, a further seven First Places were gained at various Musical Festivals throughout the area. Other members who had stage aspirations, not to be outdone, formed an equally strong Drama Group, taking part in many festivals including a Religious Festival in Durham. They also kept the village entertained with an annual three-act play, often for charity. A group of our older members formed the "Golden Belles" and entertained WI

Whorlton & Westerhope Women's Institute floral display in front of Westerhope Methodist Church Grounds.

meetings in a light-hearted way. During the 1970s and '80s, the yearly pantomime, written by one of our own members, was always a great success, both for our members and for other outside organisations when we 'took it on tour'.

The 1990s saw us 'on tour' ourselves as we became more adventuresome, enjoying trips as far north as Edinburgh and as far south as the Palace of Versailles, via Paris, with Windsor Castle, Buckingham Palace, Waddeston Manor, not forgetting Skipton, Berwick and York in between. Our loyal husbands have not always been left at home either and a tour of the Nissan Car Plant near Sunderland proved so popular, that a second visit was arranged to accommodate the numbers. We also invited them to join us one year on a visit to the Sunderland Glass Centre (pub lunch included) and a visit to the High House Farm Brewery, near the small Northumbrian village of Matfen, was one of the highlights of 2009. The farm, only a few miles from the source of the outbreak, had been badly affected by the Foot and Mouth disaster of 2001 and, like many others, had been forced to diversify or go out of business. We would like to think that our visit helped the healing process in some small way.

PRESIDENTS OF WHORLTON & WESTERHOPE WI SINCE 1930

Mrs McGee, wife of the North Walbottle Colliery Manager
Mrs Baxter, wife of the headmaster, Whorlton School
Miss Baxter, teacher
Mrs Mary Ross
Mrs Doris Alderson
Mrs Peggy Allison
Mrs Anne Laybourn
Mrs Margaret Ingram
Mrs Anne Laybourn
Mrs Audrey Dixon (the present President)

Minute Book and other records are now in the County Archives. We celebrated our 80th Anniversary in June 2010. All our members enjoyed a three-course dinner at Ryton Country Hotel. A Garden, with a commemorative plaque, was also planted with flowers in the Westerhope Methodist Church Grounds.

Apart from the churches, we are the oldest organisation in Westerhope with a growing membership and we hope to continue for many more years.

Westerhope and Whorlton WI Ladies celebrating Westerhope Village Centenary – Ann Ebblewhite, Margaret Ingram, Rene Orton, Audrey Ryan and Rita Tremble.

THE GAMES WE PLAYED

If you have a conversation with children these days, even at school holiday times, they generally come out with the expression "I'm bored". In our childhood we didn't have time to be bored, there was so much to do. Apart from the many games we played, there were so many other activities in which to be involved. We must accept however, that we did not have the constraints that children have today. We would have been horrified if either of our parents suggested accompanying us to and from school, or instructing us as to when or where to play. In addition, we did not have the lure of watching television or dabbling with computers and their associated games, nor did we have the many other benefits that today's affluence allows – family cars, excessive pocket money etc.

In contrast, we made our own amusements and there were no limits imposed on how far from the home that we could play, as long as we were back for our regular meal times, shared with the rest of the family.

Apart from organised games, many hours were taken up with playing football with either a tennis or sponge ball, with clothes put down to mark the goals and with no limit to how many players were on each side. The matches went on until it was too dark to see!

Westerhope AFC. Back row: Mr J. Lumsden, Mr N. Lumsden, Charles Clifton, Malcolm Kirk, Ernie Richardson, unknown, Alan Milburn, Jimmy Rawlinson, J. Lyle, Mr J. Hunter, Frank Dodds, Arnold Heppell. Front row: unknown, Billy Wood, Pringle, John Docherty, John Walker, Ken Williams, Raymond Ramshaw, Mr Laidler.

Left: St John's Cricket Club in the early 1900s. Jack Wilson is second from the left in the front row with Bill Ross on the opposite side with pads.

Westerhope Council School – The Tambourine Girls in the 1930s – Joyce Robson, Olive Siddon, Violet Smith, Jean Bell, Connie Brown, Audrey Brown, Vera Hall, Lilian Houstan, Mary Williams.

Although we played football throughout the year, cricket was generally restricted to the normal playing season. This was always a two-sided game, with a group playing and taking turns to bat and bowl. If we were fortunate we had stumps to bowl to, but it was more often a dustbin or merely three chalk marks on a convenient brick wall of a house or outside toilet or coal house.

Maybe one of the most popular games was marbles, played not only by children, but adults in some mining communities. In fact the British Championship, which is for adults only, takes place on Good Friday each year, at the Greyhound Public House at Tirsley Green in Sussex. Marbles took various forms, some common stone, some real marble, but in more recent times, coloured glass which were originally produced in Venice in the 15th century.

There were several games played with marbles, the most popular in our childhood being what we called 'three holey', with several rules applying.

Several other ball games were played, mostly by boys, although girls will recall the game 'Queenie, who's got the ball?'. The game 'Cannon' was also played by both boys and girls which involved throwing a ball at a tin with sticks on the top and played by two sides.

A lot of our games were played in the winter darkness, with the glow of the street lighting for illumination. In this atmosphere, the popular game was 'Mount the Cuddy'.

'*Mount the Cuddy*'.

This game was also played with two sides, with the side who lost the toss, forming the cuddy, with one child as a buffer with the others bending low against each other head to tail. The 'on' side then leapt on the cuddy with the intention of collapsing the cuddy. If they succeeded, they took another turn. If the cuddy held firm, they then reversed the role, becoming the 'on' side.

The history of these games came to light on the day of the unveiling of the Westerhope Wheel on 2nd August 2008. On the same day there was the official re-opening of the Westerhope Community Association on Hillhead Road following its re-furbishment. These two important events were followed by the Heritage Festival in the Westerhope Community Association building and grounds.

During the afternoon there were demonstrations of some traditional games including some of the following:

Mount a Cuddy	Hide and Seek
Jack Shine your Maggy	Headers
Relievo	What's in the Window
Kick the Block	Truth or Dare
Cannon	Diabloes
Geordie Canaa Cross the Watta	Chucks
Leap Frog	Yo-Yo's
Simon Says	Quoits
Hot Rice	Catapults
Tip Cat	Tops and Whips
Tiggy	Skipping
Tiggy on High	Hop Scotch
Marbles	Ball Games – Queenie etc
Follow the Leader	Hood and Gourd
Pitchy – Cigarette Cards / Milk Tops	Football
Rounders	Cricket

Additional activities we played when we were young:

Sledging	Scouts
Bogies	Girls' Brigade
Fishing – sticklebacks	Boys' Brigade
Frog spawning	Gloopers and other Clubs
Roller skating	Pea Shooters
Brownies	Catapults
Guides	Flying kites – including making them
Cubs	

Westerhope Netball team, April 1950. Back row: Elizabeth Robson, Alison Banks, Sybil Borthwick, June Charlton. Front row: Mr Peggs Headmaster, Brenda Ramshaw, June Walton, Vera Walton, Miss Baxter.

JOAN COLE (née ROSS)

Joan's father was Fred Ross, a colliery winding engine man and her mother Mary Anne Batten. They were married at Seghill Parish Church. Their first child was Anne, then Joan was born on the 27th March 1924 at home in Cramlington and christened at home because her mother was very ill for a while following childbirth.

When one year old, the family moved to Westerhope as her father started employment at Benwell Colliery. They lived in Bainbridge's Buildings, firstly in Mary Terrace, then Edna Terrace. Her father then transferred from Benwell Colliery to Caroline Colliery (the top Monty) and they came to live in 10 Thomas Street, which was one of the colliery properties known as Benson's Buildings. Benson was the colliery owner.

Joan has many childhood memories, the most outstanding was the day that the Methodist Chapel Hall was opened in 1929 when she was 5 years old. On that occasion Joan was to present a bouquet to Mrs Sanderson – Mrs France was also present and immaculately dressed as always, including her silver fox fur. Mrs France insisted that Joan should wear a Quaker outfit which her mother made. The ceremonial party included Sir John Hunter of Swan Hunter fame, who no doubt would make a donation to the Chapel, and Mr France who was a great supporter of the Chapel paying the stipend of its first Pastor – Mr Dewhurst and also purchasing a house for him.

Another occasion was when she took the part of Snow White in what was advertised as a Grand Operetta, *Snow White and the Seven Dwarfs*. It was held on Saturday, 16th March 1935 and entrance was by programme, costing sixpence each.

Other memories were Chapel trips to Tynemouth each year, when they had to walk down to Kenton Bank Foot to get the train to and from Tynemouth. Chapel Sunday School anniversaries, seeing cows being driven from Buffy's field (Buffy was the name of the France's children's pony) down Newbiggin Lane up to Turner's farm in

Opening Sunday School Hall in 1929. Left to right: Gerald France MP, Mrs Sanderson, Sir Joseph Hunter, Joan Ross presenting flowers to Gerald France MP.

North Avenue to be milked and helping her parents to make clippy mats in the winter time.

She attended Westerhope Hillhead School from 5 until she left at 14 and recalls the Headmaster Mr Reed and his staff – Messrs Laidler, Lumley and Harrison with Misses Nairn, Baxter and Pond. School friends were Jenny Freestone and Gladys Appleby.

A special annual event was when they were invited to a day of entertainment at the Miners' Institute, which included a ventriloquist and other performers. All the children were given a bun, a bag of sweets and an orange.

We all enjoyed some school games of hop scotch, mount a cuddy, skipping and tops and whips.

We also enjoyed the school camp at Berwick which lasted a week, followed by a trip to the Hoppings on the Town Moor in Race Week.

Most of us got up to childhood pranks – the popular one being a visit to Wakinshaw's orchard at the back of Runnymede to 'collect' apples and pears.

The matinees at the Picture Palace on Wednesdays and Saturdays were always well attended. The owner was Mr Longhorn and he was always present trying to subdue the noise made by the children. There was always a smoky atmosphere which I could never understand. The stalls were priced at one pence and the circle, two pence (old money).

My friends and I attended Sunday School at the Methodist Chapel and we enjoyed all of the activities there. My mother was a member of the Chapel, although until we came to Westerhope, she had always attended the Anglican Church. However, she met a Mrs Edie Rae in the village, who encouraged her to come to the Chapel as transport to St John's Church was difficult in those days. She became a member of the Women's Fellowship and the League of British Women, a strong temperance movement. As such, she campaigned strongly against the opening of the Runnymede Public House. My mother and Mrs Rae remained lifelong friends.

We loved the outings of the League of British Women, which went to Saltburn and Redcar, organised by Evelyn Wakinshaw, the Minister's daughter.

The Youth Club and Girls' Life Brigade were very popular at Chapel. Thomas and Ossie Bell together with Arnold Harris were Youth and Sunday School leaders and Mrs Marjorie Robson was the Girls' leader.

Westerhope Council School pupils performing 'Ian of Windmill Land' in the 1930s. Back row: Allan Phipps, Fred McKillip, Eric Robson, Robert Phillipson, Norman Lumsden, Harman Barrass, Arnold Heppell, Tommy Lawson. Front row: Audrey Marshall, Jean Varty, Norma Trevethick, Ruby Bainbridge, Maureen Reay, Eilene Tate, Lillian Crieghton, Marion Dawson.

When Joan left school she went to the Northern Commercial College to take a secretarial course. Her first job was at Fieldings, a New Zealand butter and cheese importer, then became employed as a secretary for the Hartley Main Colliery Company before becoming Secretary to the Duke of Northumberland's Agent in the old Eldon Square buildings for four years. Her last job was as secretary at Westerhope School from 1969 to 1989.

Then came marriage to Bob Cole (Coley), her long-term school friend – they had always been linked together. They were married at St John's (Whorlton) Church on the 28th November 1945. Joan's sister Winifred was her bridesmaid and the best man was Billy Holdsworth, Bob's brother-in-law.

Their first home was 50 Rogerson Terrace, followed by 29 Dilston Drive, 30 Bournemouth Gardens, 1 Dene Park in Darras Hall and finally 13 Aisgill Drive, Chapel House. Bob was a popular local footballer who had captained his school team, played for their Old Schoolboys before joining Throckley Welfare. He had trials for Middlesbrough FC. Bob had been employed by Vickers Armstrongs before being conscripted into the Army Dental Corps. He saw service in Singapore. He became a corporal and served for two years. Upon returning home he became an accountant with Minories Garages for thirteen years before joining Cowies of Sunderland, working particularly for Tom Cowie, their Managing Director.

Joan and Bob had two sons, Geoffrey now aged 62 years and Peter aged 52 years. Geoffrey was educated at Dame Allens School and then Manchester University from where he entered into a teaching career. Prior to teaching in England he taught English in Uganda. He and his wife Carol are currently involved in voluntary work in Cambodia. They have a daughter Laura and a son Nicholas. Peter has followed in his father's footsteps, has his own accountancy business and is married to Avril. They have two sons, Andrew and Michael, each following an accountancy career and a daughter Rachel who is also entering the accountancy profession.

Joan has led a very active social life. She has been a member of the Women's Institute for 62 years, was secretary for the Young Wives group at Chapel for five years and was treasurer for the CHADCA Ladies Club for nine years. In her younger days she had been a member of the Chapel Choir. On one occasion, she played the organ, a reminder that she had taken piano lessons from a Doris Hancock in the village for a shilling per hour.

Other memories flood in – the house shops with Mrs Powell in North Avenue selling pies and peas, Mrs Stanley in North Avenue with her sweet shop and Mrs Allison with her sweet shop in what was known as Stanley's Buildings. The front of the buildings had beautiful flower gardens with Mr Stanley giving a prize for the best kept garden. North Avenue was just a dirt track in those days.

There was the tin hut at the corner of Newbiggin Lane where several activities took place including one Brownies Group. Next to it was Ella Hart's shop – one of the first in Westerhope.

Joan's parents – Mr & Mrs Fred Ross with sister Anne, Joan in centre and sister Winifred in front.

Another event was when the Sword Dancers performed up Beaumont Terrace followed by Mrs Ellen Hewitson with her horse-drawn cart on which she had a coal fired boiler on which she made fish and chips for sale. She took this to the Hoppings every Race Week.

Then there were country walks, down Newbiggin Lane, across the fields to Kenton, through what is now Newbiggin Hall Estate and returning on the footpath to Black Swine Farm.

The memories are endless!

What an interesting and lovely village – WESTERHOPE.

CALLERTON VILLAGE

Dorothy Meek was born into real farming stock, and the family she belonged to, farmed in the Callerton area for almost a hundred years. While talking to her you could hear traces of the true Northumbrian farmer's dialect. Dorothy was born at Ponteland and, when six years old, the family moved to Callerton Grange. They lived there for twenty years, then moved to Lough House, not to be confused with Lough Bridge House, where the river Ouseburn flows under the road. Lough House Farm is next to what was old Callerton Pit.

There is quite a lot of folk lore attached to this expanse of farmland, which stretched from south of the River Pont and Ponteland to Stamfordham Road. Lough Bridge House was originally 'The White Swan Pub'. Dorothy Meek told me the names of the two Loughs, which are "Foster's Lough" – the one near the bridge, and "Sharper's Lough" further up the road. The Meek family moved to Lough House Farm in 1935 so she knew quite a lot about the area and became very annoyed when someone called the "Loughs" the Callerton Ponds. While ploughing in one of the fields, her brother dug into what they thought could have been an old Cockpit. The fields are honeycombed with old pit shafts and wagon ways, which can still be clearly seen, although they may go back to the 17th or 18th century. Most of these shafts would be the shallow "Bell Pits", maybe worked by monks who are known to have travelled from Tynemouth to Cheeseburn Grange, Wylam and Swinburn.

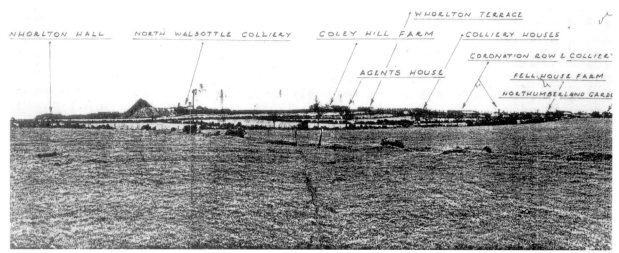

North Walbottle Panoramic View from Callerton Ponds locally called Loughs (Small Lakes). The lakes are the source of the Ouseburn which flows under Callerton bridge down to the River Tyne. Their names "Fosters" "Lough" – the nearest to the bridge and "Sharper's Lough" – further up the road across the fields.

After the Second World War, the NCB sank a drift, which was supposed to pick up coal that was left in North Walbottle Colliery. The seams of coal get thinner near the surface, ("come to bank" as the miner says). That is why you will find traces of coal for miles around this area, in fact during the 1921-26 miners' strikes, coal was being sold for 1/6 a ton from the local fields. The NCB pulled down a cottage, which was known locally as Percy Watson's. Evidently he was the last person to live there, and nearby was a spot, according to Dorothy Meek, called "Mount Holy", which seems to suggest connections with the monks who travelled this way. An ivy-covered tree can be seen marking that vicinity today.

Many years went by before they had a bus service. The people had to come to Westerhope to shop and share our "Picture Palace". They belonged to Castle Ward, not Newburn UDC as we did. Their nearest pint was the Jingling Gate but quite a few were members of the Westerhope Excelsior Club. It wasn't till after the First World War that they got their very own "Army Hut" social club, and some of the founders were Westerhope men. One Callerton boy, Jack Kerrigan, who attended Whorlton School, left at 14 to start a mining career at North Walbottle Colliery. He later became a Councillor and eventually became Lord Mayor of Newcastle.

Godfrey Watson, in his book *Good Wife Hot* explains the origins of the Callerton name, which seem to have names which have connections with the Delavals.

CALLERTON is the hill where calves were grazed.

THERE WERE THREE CALVERDONS: The first known as Black Callerton, came from outcrops of coal around it and it was CALVERDON DELAVALE.

CALVERDON DE VALENCE was called after the family who owned part of what is now High Callerton.

CALVERDON D'ARREYNS is where the name DARRAS HALL came from and he also tells us that the land stretching from the RIVER PONT southward was once called CALLERTON BY THE WATER.

When North Walbottle was established as housing for miners, there was an additional need for houses. Mr Severs, the colliery manager and Mr Morton, a director of the colliery company, decided to build houses near to the colliery and so developed Callerton Village with Severs Terrace and Morton Crescent.

They have attractive gardens at their front and Callerton Village has been very successful for several years, in the 'Britain in Bloom' awards.

HISTORY OF NEWBIGGIN HALL

The history of the lands on which the Newbiggin Hall is built goes back to 1166, when it was called Newbiggin-on-the-Moor. It was part of the great Barony in the North East, including such well known places as Gosforth, Newburn and Whalton along with Alnwick, Morpeth, Mitford, Bolam and Callerton. It was called the Whalton Barony and it appears that in 1205, King John was responsible for handing out these parcels of land to the Feudal Lords of the country. In 1329, the Barony was broken up, but kept together with Denton, Fawdon and Kenton by the Widdrington Family. Other well known names appeared when, in 1350, John Denton acquired a piece of land at Newbiggin-on-the-Moor.

Then later, big land owners were erecting fences around what was known as common pasture lands and the owners of small holdings were being prosecuted for using what they had known as their property. Many of

Front view of the hall which had extensive gardens

the rights of way footpaths were being ploughed over, which still occurs today.

In those early days, coal would be dug up by the so called bell pits, where a hole was dug out and broadened as they found near surface coal seams. A ladder was dropped down and the miner worked there until lack of ventilation forced him to pull up his ladder and move to another nearby spot. A Mr Hudson was a technical expert in mining and gave advice on local mining. He lived in a large house on the site of the Newbiggin Hall we know. He died in 1700. He must have been wealthy because when he died, he left £10 in his will for the widows and orphans of Newbiggin.

When Newbiggin Hall was demolished, a stone lintel was found with the date 1794 which proved that the Hudson House had been replaced. After the Hudson family, on to the moor came such well known families as the Rogers, Rokebys and Montagus, who were keenly interested in mining. Another name linked to coal

Newbiggin Hall was built in 1794

mining was Richard Peck. He was a mining engineer and lived in the large stone house on the corner where Newbiggin Lane turns right to Kenton Bank Foot. Before 1826, Matthew Bell of Wolsington and his son were living at Newbiggin House. It was while the Bells were living there that it became known as Newbiggin Hall. The family also farmed at Whorlton Grange (the present golf course). One of the sons was quite wild and was known to come galloping through the village on horseback. Colonel James Reed JP came to the Hall after Henry Bell in 1887, followed by John Watson-Spencer of Newburn steelworks fame. He left in 1906 and died in 1908.

Newbiggin Hall in 1930. Staff of Mr & Mrs Gerald France. Second left Bowden Parker 'Chauffeur', Jimmy Ames 'Gardener'.

The France family came from Horsley Hall to Newbiggin Hall in 1909. Mr. and Mrs. Gerald France had a family of four sons and one daughter and the whole family was soon involved in the social life of the village. Mr France had been a Liberal MP in Richmond, Yorkshire, from 1910 to 1918. He was a director of several companies in Newcastle including Scott and Turners (Andrew Liver Salts) and Nestles. Other interests were the Boys' Brigade, Poor Children's Homes' Association and temperance movements. As a regular visitor to Westerhope School, he brought a supply of his firm's chocolate, which made him very popular. The village children were often entertained at the Hall, especially during the miners' strikes. Through his naval service in the First World War he became a personal friend of Admiral Jellicoe, who visited the Hall during the 1920s.

Mrs France's father was T.H. Bainbridge of Eshott Hall, son of the founder of Bainbridges. Gerald France died in 1935. He had been a great friend to the village and to the Methodist Church in particular. Following his death, Mrs France purchased the land surrounding the Hall to safeguard the privacy of her home.

During the Second World War, the Hall was used as an RAF hospital. After the war the Hall was sold to Mr Charles Lee and the farm to Mr James Moorhouse. Mr Lee sold the Hall to Newcastle Breweries who converted it to a residential public house. While performing at the Newcastle Empire in the mid-1960s the Beatles stayed there. Sadly the Hall was eventually burnt down.

The whole area surrounding the Hall was finally purchased by the Newcastle upon Tyne City Council for this massive council owned housing development on the Newbiggin Hall Estate.

A booklet entitled *SHIFTING – a history of Newbiggin Hall Estate 1960-1988* was published by the Newbiggin Hall Local History Society in 1989.

GERMAN PLANE CRASH

What a dreadful night! Newcastle was undergoing a German air raid. Down the road at Slatyford the 'ack-ack' battery was in action with searchlights sweeping the sky. Our fighters were also in action, repelling the German bombers which had swept in over the North Sea.

Air Raid Wardens and other emergency services were on the alert when, suddenly, out of the sky came this German plane, losing height rapidly and then this tremendous crash in the fields of Coley Hill Farm.

Emergency services rushed into action, some from the First Aid Post which was within the Hillhead School, and several Home Guard personnel. They found the crew, one of whom was dead (he had tried to bale out) and another injured. The pilot attempted to destroy the plane with an explosive charge, but was prevented from doing this.

The wreckage of the Heinkel 111.

The crew were then taken to the Miners' Institute which was the Civil Defence Headquarters, given first aid and some refreshments. The pilot was Hauptmann Eugen Eichler, the navigator was Feldwebel Franz Olsson and the wireless operator was Obergefreiter Wilhelm Koch. The air gunner was Gefreiter Hans Schiealinski. They were soon removed from the area.

Mr Martin Greenfield, who lived in Chatsworth Gardens, was a Chief Technician with the RAF, and was called to the scene to inspect the plane and he later confirmed some of the details.

It was revealed that this was a prototype plane. Until that time, the furthest their planes could fly was to the Manchester area. The plane had flown as far as Glasgow, which was confirmed in the report by the RAF pilot in his account of how he shot down the Heinkel 111 5F/KG4 plane on the 6th May 1941 at 3.00 hours.

Members of the crew were eventually sent to a prisoner of war camp in Bowmanville, Ontario, Canada.

There are many and varied opinions regarding the position of the crash, but apparently the plane could be seen from the gate heading to the Hillhead School which suggests that the site would be 100 yards from the rear of the Miners' Institute, now the Westerhope Community Association, on Hillhead Road.

Left: Two miners, Thomas Dawson and Ernest Stoker, members of the Home Guard, showing how they captured members of the crew of the bomber by using a piece of metal from the plane as a revolver. They subsequently handed them over to the police. Left to right: Thomas Dawson, Mrs Laidler (née Martha Llewelyn, Mrs Steve Rigby, Ernest (Ernie) Stoker, Mrs Taylor & daughter June. Lady half hidden not known.

GERMAN PLANE CRASH – PILOT'S REPORT

May 5-6 1941 at 3.00 hours Sergeant G.L. Lawrence's (Pilot) RAF account of contacting and shooting down Heinkel 111 5F + ./KG4 at North Walbottle.

The Heinkel crashed at North Walbottle in the early hours of the 6th May 1941. The aircraft had dropped bombs on Greenock and was a few miles south-west of Glasgow when it was attacked at 01.44 hours by a Defiant night fighter (T4943) of 141 Squadron, Ayr, crewed by Sergeant G.L. Lawrence (Pilot) and Sergeant Hithersay (Gunner).

Lawrence's report of the incident describes what happened.

"On the night of 5-6th May 1941, I was ordered off to patrol according to vectors at midnight. I was airborne at 00.04 hours on the 6th and was controlled by Vandyke for the first 30 minutes then switched over to GCI, being controlled by them until I was forced to ask for a homing vector because of a faulty microphone and lack of petrol; I only had 15 gallons left. I was given a vector of 120 degrees, which brought to the coast at 12,000 feet a few miles south of Greenock and was asked to call Vandyke for further homing vectors.

"Shortly after receiving a vector for 140 degrees from Vandyke, my gunner, Sgt Hithersay, saw a twin-engined aircraft some 300 yards behind and some 200 yards to port, flying on a parallel course and silhouetted against some cloud lit up by incendiaries on the ground.

"I throttled back to 20 mph IAS to allow the aircraft to overtake me. It came up to within 100 yards then altered course and passed behind to my starboard and, when next seen by me, was some 200 yards away to my beam, flying due south. I recognised the aircraft as a Heinkel 111 and closed in rapidly, intending to take up my position slightly ahead of and to port of the enemy aircraft but my gunner opened fire at approximately 150 yards with a three-second burst while I was still to beam slightly below. Some of these rounds could be seen striking the fuselage near the tail. The next two bursts, from 50 yards and point blank range, raked the length of the fuselage and port engine.

"The De Wilde (an explosive incendiary .303 bullet) ammunition could be seen exploding very plainly. The enemy aircraft then started doing steep turns to port and starboard and I endeavoured to formate, keeping slightly ahead and below while my gunner was firing when he could, all bursts being at short range."

Right: This photograph contains members of the crew that crashed at North Walbottle in 1941. The KG4 personnel were in POW Camp 30, Bowmanville, Ontario, Canada, in 1942. Hauptmann Eugen Eichler, pilot, is first from the left on the front row.

It was exactly one year later that a German Bomber flew over the area, presumably intending to destroy the Vicker's Armstrong's factory. It was a cloudy night, but there must have been a break in the clouds when the crew saw what they must have thought was the river, but were the gleaming railway lines, running from North Walbottle Colliery to Lemington. They dropped their bombs, destroying part of Coley Hill Terrace, killing William Musgrave the colliery locomotive driver, his daughter Irene, aged 20 years, and their neighbour Margaret Allen.

THE GAUNTLET

This was a newspaper containing local news and articles of interest produced by local churches in the mid-1970s. It was widely circulated, was free, but donations were accepted. Local people were able to submit articles and local tradesmen advertised their products.

One contributor was Mr Desmond Walton, who had articles published on a variety of historical features and buildings.

When *The Gauntlet* ceased publication, a lot of local history was lost, but fortunately, Desmond kept a scrap book which he passed on to me which has been invaluable.

The following are three of the many features:

COFFEE JOHNNY

Coffee Johnny (also known in places as Coffee Tommy) was born about 1867. His real name was John William Herdman. He was believed to have worked on the formation of Gosforth Park Racecourse in the 1880s, but took to the roads after a disappointment in his love life.

He was a remarkable figure, with soles and heels on his boots about three inches thick, having nailed on soles and heels from 'throw outs'. He also had several layers of clothing and a bowler hat.

Over his shoulder was a small bundle containing his towel etc, as he would bathe himself in a burn or stream.

An oil painting of Johnny was on show in Blayney's the wine merchant's window when they were in business in Grainger Street.

One might ask how did he live?

His regular route extended anywhere between Belsay, Ponteland, Morpeth, South Gosforth, Kenton and along the countryside north of the Tyne to Heddon. There were many farms along the route in those days. A pot of tea and a sandwich was all he asked and people were generally kind to him.

There was an occasion when he was asked why he didn't find work. This was about noon. He replied "Why ivvory body wud be hevin thor dinners".

"Well why not try just after one o'clock."

"Why neebody starts work in the afternuen," he retorted.

"Why not try first thing in the mornin' then".

"Ah divvent like gettin' up in the mornin" said Johnny. Bed for him would probably be in a stable or hay shed.

When admitted to hospital in 1926 after being knocked down by a car, he was wearing five coats, twelve pairs of braces, nine shirts, five pairs of socks and his shoes had nine layers of leather or rubber – and of course his bowler or – dutt as it was called.

Coffee Johnny.

FISH ANNIE

Annie was one of the Cullercoats fishwives who travelled throughout Tyneside, with a creel on their backs full of their catch. Very little is known of her but she was a regular visitor to Westerhope, sometimes setting up a stall at the end of one of the terraces. She would travel from Cullercoats to Kenton Bank Foot station and then walk up Newbiggin Lane to Westerhope. Her cry would be for lobsters, crabs, willicks or caller herring, twelve a penny. Some housewives tried to get more herring for their penny, but she was heard to say that "I would rather throw them over the dyke than sell them cheaper". What a tiring trail it would be back to Cullercoats. She would have probably lived in one of the fisherman's cottages, which should never have been demolished.

Left: Local character Fish Annie.

CATCHEM JOHN

John Dickinson and his wife lived in Primrose Cottage. It was probably one of the first cottages to be built in Westerhope. It dates back to the 1860s and was built for the farm hind who worked for the Red Cow Farm, on the opposite side of Stamfordham Road.

John got his nickname from chasing children who mimicked him, as he had a quick unusual walk and also had a speech impediment.

He was a popular character, quite 'well off' and owned three racehorses – Gallowgate Lad, Primrose Ben and Gingerbread – which he kept in a stable next to the Cobbler's Corner shop.

When the founders of Westerhope met at the Red Cow Farm site, he often provided them with a cup of tea.

Mrs Dickinson is the lady who appears on the front of the 'BYGONE WESTERHOPE' booklet, standing with the child at Primrose Cottage.

Right: Mr & Mrs Dickinson of Primrose Cottage – Catchem John.

MAUREEN LAIDLER (née LENAGHAN)

I was born on 5th February 1939 in 5 Greenfield Avenue and moved to 8 Ellesmere Avenue when I was one year old, I was christened at the English Martyr's Church in Fenham, where my parents were married.

My father's name was John Lenaghan and he was born in Benwell on the 23rd June 1909. My mother's name was Ellen Bulford and she was born in Callerton Village on the 1st February 1913. I was their only child.

Father was employed at North Walbottle Colliery and eventually became a coal cutter. Later, he moved to Caroline Colliery (the Top Monty). He finally worked at the Havannah Drift Mine until he became Union Representative for the miners.

He also became a Labour Councillor for the Westerhope Ward on the Newburn Urban District Council and had the distinction of becoming Mayor of Newburn.

My father always took a pride in being involved in the Miners' Institute (the 'Tute') on Hillhead Road, having been there at its opening ceremony in 1925. When the ownership of the Institute was transferred from the miners to Newcastle City Council in 1977, he was involved in the negotiations and an article was published in the press regarding this, together with his photograph. A plaque is displayed within the building, dedicated to John Lenaghan for his services to the community.

Councillor John Lenaghan – Mayor of Newburn.

I attended Westerhope School on Hillhead Road and I recall my Headmaster, Mr Reed followed by Mr Peggs and the teachers – Miss Baxter, Miss Nairn and Miss Stephenson. My school friends were Joan Crosby and Norah Williams. When I left the school I went to Skerry's College to take a secretarial course.

During my schooldays I enjoyed the games we played – hop scotch, skipping, hide and seek and the local nature walks – the blue bell dene, the bridle path and across the golf course.

I enjoyed reading books, my favourites being The Famous Five and books on history. At this time I also took piano lessons from Mrs Bell who lived in Briarside.

I only have vague recollections of wartime, but I was conscious of food rationing, particularly sweet rationing, but do remember the huge bonfire down by Kensington Villas on VE Day. There was also a celebration with a brass band playing at the junction of Beaumont Terrace and Stamfordham Road.

I loved Westerhope Village and recall all of the shops – Mrs Bright at the Post Office, Harry Dunn and Basil Hall, the butchers, Tommy Metcalf the barber, Teasdales the bakers, Aylens the newsagents, Mr Cross at Cyclemiles, the Hadrian next door, Allans Store with proprietors Rachel and Lena Wilson and lastly the Co-op with those big barrels of cheese and best butter etc. Harris's gardens were always a feature at the end of the village, with their main products – tomatoes, chrysanthemums and spring flowers. I must not miss out the ORION, the cinema with its sweets and ice cream kiosk at the entrance and its popular matinees.

At 16, I put my secretarial course to good use by being employed at HARKERS, a well-known furniture store in Grainger Street and eventually becoming personal assistant to their buyer.

When I started work, I often went to the Saturday evening dances at the Miners' Institute, where I met my husband to be, Jim Laidler. He lived at West Denton and was an apprentice electrician at North Walbottle Colliery. When he completed his apprenticeship, he went to work at Newcastle Breweries for several years as a Service Engineer and followed in that capacity at other companies.

Following our courtship, we were married at the English Martyr's Church on 8th June 1958. Our daughter Karen was born in 1961 and our son Christopher in 1965. They both live locally – Karen in Langdon Road and Christopher in Abbey Farm. We lived in Whorlton Grange but later moved into our present home, a bungalow on Wedmore Road, Hillheads.

Jim has lived a very active married life, being a playing member of Westerhope Golf Club and for many years looked after the Club's Junior Golf Team and encouraged many juniors to play golf. In addition, he was a Manager of some very successful junior football teams playing at the Westerhope Community Association Sports Ground.

Two other notable members of my family were my Uncle Alfred Bulford who was a prisoner of war in Germany in the 1939-45 war who returned home and was on the Parish Council at St John's (Whorlton) Church for many years and my 'Uncle' Chas Woods, who was a Newburn Urban District Labour Councillor. Among other interests he was a keen golfer and was President of the Westerhope Golf Club from 1957 until 1978.

It was on the 20th October 1962 that a grand ceremony took place at the Golf Club when the new club house was officially opened. 'Uncle' Chas officiated at that ceremony.

Right: The successful Westerhope Community Centre football team. Front row, left to right: Paul Ovenden, Terry Baines, Kevin Nicholson, Chris Laidler, Darren Brown. Back row: Jim Laidler (manager), Carlos Park, Robbie Park, Neil Chipwell, Mark Kenny and Jim Gellatly (coach).

A newspaper article at the time told the story of this cup winning side:

"The Westerhope Community Centre team have won the NAYC Blackburn Trophy for under-14 sides without conceding a goal in their three matches.

In the five-a-side tournament at Gosforth High School, they beat Blaydon 1-0, Longbenton 2-0 and John Boste 4-0.

The team are part of an under-14 team managed by Jim Laidler and coached by Jim Gellaty. They play in the Tyneside and District Colts League and their success include winning the West Division Shield and Presidents Cup. They were also runners-up in the League Cup.

And the under-13 side has won the Westerhope Shield in a five-a-side competition at Montagu and North Fenham Boy's Club.'

WESTERHOPE SWORD DANCERS

Until the 1930s, sword dancing was a common form of recreation in mining villages and North Walbottle Sword Dancers made a major contribution towards the popularity of this sport. They formulated many different sequences and a Mr Cecil Sharp, the famous old song collector and the founder of the then modern Morris and Sword Dancing sequences, referred to the expertise of the miners at North Walbottle. Several teams were raised from Westerhope Hillhead School around 1926 and in that year, fielded four teams in the Newcastle Music Tournament. The North Walbottle Sword Dance is performed by Morris Dancers throughout Britain and has been welcomed by the Union of English Morris Dance Clubs.

The Westerhope team was British Champions and appeared for one week at the Palladium in London. During that week, they were approached to go on tour in America, but they declined the offer – their response being that they were coal miners and if they were away for more than a week they would lose their jobs and consequently their free rent and house coal.

In a final conversation with Henry Smith, I asked him if he had ever seen the group dancing. His reply was that they performed just before Race Week up and down Beaumont Terrace, followed by Mrs Ellen Hewitson. She had a horse drawn flat cart, on which she had a coal-fired oven, on which she made fish and chips for sale. The following week, she made her appearance at the 'hoppings', selling her fish and chips. She was Mrs Ellen Hewitson and this was the foundation of the Hewitson haulage business in West Avenue.

Westerhope Sword Dancers in 1919. Standing: Sam Taylor, Frank Lee, Jimmy Bland, Jimmy Hall. Sitting: Jimmy Hannant, John Hall (Melodian), Ishmael Jarvis. Their proficiency and reputation allowed them to dance professionally for short periods, performing all over the country. Christmas was particularly busy, dancing around country houses in the area, Stella, Dissington and Wellington. The team's "Rappers", (Swords) were the gift of the Lady Brown of Benwell and the Duke of Northumberland referred to them as 'His' Sword Dancers.

PUBLIC HOUSES AND CLUBS

Although many shops were erected in the early 1900s, it was obvious that there were no public houses or clubs. The reason was that the Northern Allotment Society had specified in the deeds of the house owners, that no public houses selling alcohol were allowed, pigs could not be kept, or pawnshops opened within the area.

The nearest public house was the Jingling Gate (originally called the Gingling Gate) which dated back to the late 1600s. In addition to the 'ale house' it also had a smithy, which was useful for the many horse drawn vehicles which called there. The blacksmith, who was there until the smithy closed, was Dick Oliver, a very popular character.

To overcome the public house embargo, a Working Men's Club was started in Dene House, Stamfordham Road, but due to robberies, it soon closed. A new club was started in Wheatfield Road in an old farmhouse in 1910.

Finally, a new club – the Excelsior Working Men's Club was built on an adjacent site on Wheatfield

The Jingling Gate in 1916.

Road in 1935. It is very popular now and apart from selling alcohol, it provides varied forms of entertainment, attracting crowds from outside areas.

In 1947, Newcastle Breweries purchased the former home of the initiator of the Northern Allotment Society, Mr. Joseph Wakinshaw, who had built and lived in 'Runnymede' – a large stone house with extensive gardens and orchard.

Following a public enquiry, they overcame the restrictive covenant and converted 'Runnymede' into a public house, but retained the name.

In 1964 the building was demolished and a new building was erected alongside the old one.

A number of residents had united in employing a barrister to resist the purchase by Newcastle Breweries and, more especially, to prevent the sale of alcohol on the premises. A limited number of them were compensated for the covenant reversal – those immediately adjacent to the original 'Runnymede'.

The Jingling Gate has seen remarkable changes in recent years, the most recent being the erection of a large conservatory on the side providing additional restaurant facilities. It is very popular for business lunches and has proved to be attractive to the younger generation.

There is now a public house on the Hillhead Estate – 'The Hillheads'.

As a result of a number of social problems the 'Runnymede' was closed, then demolished, and the site cleared. The site is now occupied by an 'Aldi' store.

A modern view of the Jingling Gate public House.

HOME GUARD

Our Home Guard was formed shortly after the outbreak of the war. Its headquarters were the Scout Hut at the top of Wheatfield Road.

On the group photograph shown outside the Orion, seventy-two members are shown. The question has been asked 'why weren't they in the regular army' as most of them are young enough to be 'called up'. The reason was, that the majority were employed at local mines and anyone working in the coal industry or in productive engineering, were controlled by the Essential Works Order and was exempt from conscription.

The Commanding Officer had been a Captain in the Northumberland Fusiliers as early as 1898. He was Captain Ernest Miller Watts of 'Granville', Highfield Road, Westerhope. He was obviously well qualified, having joined 'The Fifths' in 1898 and had been on active service throughout the Boer War 1899-1902. On completion of his Colonial Service he saw active service in India in 1913, returning home to re-equip for service in France in 1915. He was wounded and mentioned in despatches in the First World War.

Ernest served with 'A' Company (Westerhope) Northumbrian Area Home Guard, from its formation until its disbandment. He was no Captain Mainwaring, but some of the activities had a resemblance to Dad's Army. There was a tennis court at the rear of the Methodist Church which they destroyed by digging trenches in it, for protection in the event of an attack. One of the members was firing an 'EY' Discharger – a rifle with a cup at the end to house a mills bomb. When he fired it the rifle butt fell off. Another member took his rifle home to clean the bore with a 'pull through' – a soft plug with a cord attached to it. It got stuck in the bore, couldn't remove it, so poured methylated spirits down the bore and lit it. It eventually cleared, but imagine the condition of the bore afterwards. There was always chaos in the various manoeuvres around the Newbiggin Hall estate, reminiscent of Pike and his associates.

Other officers supporting Captain Watts (ranks unknown) were Messrs Cotterill, Green and Heaton. The sergeant major was Martin Calvert, the sergeant Tommy Wheeler and one of the corporals was called Blake

Westerhope Home Guard in 1941.

Callerton Home Guard outside North Walbottle pit yard around 1942. Included are: Harry Burns, John Alexander, J. Grey, Bushy Burns and Roley Burns.

"Wor Home Guard"

A poem composed by Mrs Watts wife of Captain E.M. Watts and set to the tune of 'Blaydon Races'

Forst ye get an armband, then a service cap,
Then ye get a pull-through – then a rifle strap.
Next ye get a pair of beuts, and when ye get your gun
Yor aal set and ready for any kind of fun.

Chor
Why its champion, it makes ye fit and hard,
Marching roond the country lanes wi' wor Home Guards.
Why it's champion when it's freezing hard
At midneet when we man the Posts wi wor Home Guards.

Wi' luck ye'll get a great – coat or mebbe a cape,
And when ye get your battle dress it winnit fit your shape.
But little things don't' worry us when waiting for the Hun.
For we're aal set and ready for any kind of fun.

Second chor
Why it's champion, it makes ye fit and hard
Marching roond the country lanes wi' wor Home Guard.
Why it's champion, the syreen blaain' hard.
Howay me lads and bring yor guns thet want the Home Guards.

Just across the North Sea there is a gangster man
Who said he's wipe us off the map, but we divv'nt think he can.
Because we've got a fighting Navy and some lads in Air Force blue,
An Army brave and wor Home Guards to see the matter through.

Third chor
Oh' ye daft lad Adolph, we know ye schemed quite hard.
But ye didn't seem to reckon on wor Home Guards.
So come Adolph, ye'll find invasion hard.
For waiting here to welcome you is WOR HOME GUARD

PAT'S STORY

I was born on the 30th July 1931 at my grandparents' house on the outskirts of Westerhope. Their name was Grant and they had a smallholding which was a pig breeding farm with approximately 100 pigs. In addition, they kept a few stock beasts with always a cow for milk, plus hens, rabbits and a horse. I remember Gypsy caravans used to pitch nearby, just before the 39-45 war and they stayed there for a couple of weeks before the Hoppings began in Race Week.

Towards the end of the war, granddad had a German prisoner of war working for him. His name was Wilhelm and he was from the prisoner of war camp at Darras Hall. He was brought every morning by army lorry, and returned early evening. By that time, my grandparents farmed at Heddon with my Uncle Alec remaining at the smallholding. At Heddon they had Italian prisoners of war working for them. These prisoners were very grateful for the kindness they received and made Christmas presents for them out of wood. One of the prisoners from an adjoining farm at Heddon, stayed in the area after the war and started a very successful ice cream business.

My dad's name was Robert Wright, and my mam's was Jenny Grant and they were married at St John's (Whorlton) Church in 1929.

Dad was in the Merchant Navy in both peace and wartime and this was his lifetime career. He had the misfortune to be shot by a German soldier when he was in the Naval Division in France in the 14-18 war. I still have his Atlantic Medal but

Pat with friends Mary Sharp (Laws) and Jean Sharp (Wilson) on a motor cycle.

his others sadly were lost at sea. Dad died at 66 years of age, collapsing as he was preparing to go back to sea.

Mam had been a nursemaid and continued to live at the smallholding. She was a very active lady, helped around the smallholding and could be seen at times motorcycling around the fields. She was a devout Christian, worshipping every Sunday morning at Westerhope Methodist Church and at the Women's Fellowship on a Wednesday afternoon. Mam and dad eventually had a cottage in West Avenue. She died at the age of 101 years.

I was christened at the church where mam and dad were married, but at the age of three, used to be carried piggy back to Sunday School at Westerhope Methodist Church. I enjoyed Sunday School with the anniversaries, trips to the coast in the summer and parties at Christmas. At 14, I left school and became a member of the Young Ladies Class attending for 12 years until it disbanded because, by then, most of us were mums with young children. We regrouped years later as a Young Wives Group and many of us still meet regularly as a Wives and Friends Group, with arranged speakers.

Another activity I loved was the Girls Life Brigade which I will refer to later.

I attended Cowgate School until I was 14. During the war I was evacuated, but only to Heddon, to stay with my grandparents, so I was very fortunate. I suppose I was evacuated because of the raids over our area. There was an army camp opposite where we lived, which housed four big ack-ack guns. During raids we could hear the order to fire and our house shook when the shells were fired.

Life on the farm was great, with all of the animals and all the activities, including riding on the hay boggies. All of my friends loved to visit the farm because of the animals. They also enjoyed riding on my motor bike.

My Uncle Alec was very experienced on a motor bike and rode for the Newcastle Diamonds at Brough Park in the late '40s and early '50s. He was very popular and his son and grandson followed in the tradition, both riding for the Berwick Bandits. My uncle always rode in black leathers under the name of Farmer Grant.

I left school and became Secretary to the Manager of the Station Hotel in Newcastle. I later became a Secretary at West Denton High School for 17 years.

When I was at the Station Hotel I met some interesting personalities including Rex Harrison, the film star, Jimmy Hill the football star and Peter Brough, the famous ventriloquist with his dummy, Archie Andrews.

I met my husband-to-be Ron in, of all places, a bus queue and we courted for five years until we married at the Westerhope Methodist Church in 1952. We were married for 59 years until Ron died in 2009.

Alec (Farmer) Grant of Newcastle Diamonds Speedway team at Brough Park.

He worked as a draughtsman at Vickers Armstrongs, receiving a long service watch before he left to work for the engineering company, Ingersoll Rand.

Throughout the years we had some lovely holidays together, particularly our honeymoon, which we enjoyed in the Isle of Man at the time of the TT Motor Bike races. There were several overseas holidays and we loved cruising.

One incident I remember, was that there was a large pond near to our smallholding, where the local miners used to swim on Sunday afternoons. One afternoon, a young man got into difficulties and his brother rushed to save him. Sadly, they both drowned. My mother was just a young girl at the time, but needless to say, we were never allowed to even paddle in that pond!

Writing is possibly my main lifetime hobby. During my schooldays I had two pen friends. One was from Texas, USA, who visited me in 1976. My mam and I visited her in 1977 and 1978. Sadly, she died in 1992 after corresponding for 50 years. My other pen friend lives in Poland and we still continue our correspondence to one another.

I have had a book of poems published. I have also written stories for magazines. One of my last poems was about the 'WESTERHOPE WHEEL'.

The Girls' Brigade in 1943 – 6th Newcastle Group. The Girls' Brigade met on Friday evening in the Methodist Chapel Hall.

DENTON HALL

Although Denton Hall is not in the Westerhope Ward, it is historically linked with Westerhope Village. From an architectural viewpoint it is unique, for when it was built in 1622 for the well-known Errington family, it was the first manor house in the north of England to be without fortifications. Eventually it came into the ownership of Edward Montagu, who was born in Newcastle in 1692. It was left to him on the death of his cousin John Rogers, his share being the East Denton estate, which included nine farms – Scotswood, Woodhouse Bridge, Stoney Lee, Denton Hall, Low Hotch Pudding, High Hotch Pudding, Red Cow and Black Swine. The estate also included several coal mines, two of which were the View Pit (Low Monty) and the Caroline Pit (High Monty). In 1742, he married Elizabeth Robinson, said to be a very beautiful London socialite and founder of the Blue Stocking Club.

Edward died in 1775 and so, following his death, Elizabeth travelled north to view the estate she had inherited. As she wandered around the estate, she couldn't understand why there were so many black children around, until she was informed that they were children who worked in her mines, from as young as seven years of age. She also saw the poverty of their families, so she arranged a feast for them at the Hall. However, she became so concerned at their drunken behaviour that, instead, she had a beast roasted and arranged for a 'piece of meat' to be taken to each family per week. She recorded that on one evening, she had fifty-nine boys and girls in her courtyard to be fed on boiled beef and rice pudding. She also helped the families with their clothing.

She owned the estate for twenty-five years and as she had no family, she persuaded her nephew, Matthew Robinson, to change his name so that he could become her heir and assume the name and arms of the Montagu family. He became Lord Rokeby (a name identified with the public house which stood in the Blakelaw area). Mrs Montagu died in 1800 having lived a very colourful life in Denton Hall, where she entertained not only the local families, but many notabilities of her day. One particular notability was Silky the Ghost who appeared to many of the Hall's guests at dead of night.

The historical link between Denton Hall and Westerhope is of course, the Black Swine and Red Cow farms. As mentioned in the section Westerhope Village, the area was initially called the Red Cow Farm estate.

Reference to the Montagu View Pit (the Low Monty) – this is the pit which had that terrible disaster in 1925, when an inrush of water from the nearby Paradise pit resulted in 38 men and boys perishing in the underground workings.

WESTERHOPE LOCAL HISTORY SOCIETY

It was in 1981 when a group of 35 local residents met in West Denton School under the guidance of Mr Desmond Walton, to discuss the formation of a History Society. The meeting was in favour and adopted the name of West Newcastle Local History Society. The meetings would take place in the West Denton High School.

However, at the Annual General Meeting in May 1984 it was decided to change the name to Westerhope Local History Society and the venue to be Westerhope Methodist Church. At a meeting in May 1989 Tom Peacock was appointed Chairman having just joined the Society in the previous year. The first item on the agenda was that of the declining membership which had at one stage reached 32. (In year 2009-2010 it has reached 115.)

Two of the outstanding ventures in which we have been involved were firstly, when we celebrated the centenary of the establishment of Methodism in the village in

Westerhope Centenary Celebration Local History Society Event in 1991. Left to right: Councillor Bob Morgan, Tom Peacock (Chairman), Joe Allison, Doug Henderson (Newcastle North MP), Desmond Walton.

1901. The festival comprised a display of flower arrangements in the Church and the History Society mounted a display of photographs in the hall. During the two days of the Exhibition in excess of 900 visitors attended.

This was followed in 1995 by an exhibition of photographs and memorabilia to celebrate the centenary of the completion of the original Methodist Church and its inclusion in the plan of the Dilston Road Circuit. Another feature of the Society has been the outings we have enjoyed which have been organised by Sheila and Ron Handley. We have received support from the Westerhope Ward Committee and the Community Foundation for some of our outings.

Our meetings are held at 7.00 pm on the third Monday of each month from September to May inclusive. The talks are generally illustrated and the subjects are varied.

Left: Members of the Society at Eden Camp. We also visited places of local interest including: the Victoria Tunnel, Leazes Park, the Lit & Phil and the Mining Institute.

Westerhope by Greta Robson, 1983

Not so many years ago
When life was good, the pace was slow,
Westerhope, a village fair
Was something quite beyond compare.

The land was tilled by horse and plough
The place what then was named Red Cow.
Now on the spot there is "The Square"
(Who would have thought a farm stood there?)

Northern Allotment Society
Came out of town to see –
They were Messrs, Dickinson and Wakinshaw
Telford, Clark and several more.

The possibilities were fine.
In the year of 1889.
Houses were built, still to be seen
Are Primrose Cottage, Kendal Green.

The Chapel was built later on
Of stone and timber, fine and strong
With clock tower that was so rare
No other like it anywhere.

Where Chatsworth is, there was a pond
With orchards and green fields beyond
Newbiggin Hall stood alone –
Sir Gerald France's Stately home.

Robson's milk was kept in churns.
No bottles then and no returns.
Professional men and their abode
In the secluded Highfield Road.

Sam Piper owned the Picture Hall
The films were enjoyed by all.
Mr Witty had the Barber's Shop
Opposite the Co-op.

He was the local fire brigade
When fire broke out, he was delayed
His customers he could not fail
Before he ran out with his hose and pail.

Many men worked at the pit
Were tired and black after their shift.
The Minister lived at Runneymede
And rules were laid down in the Deed.

At Black Swine Farm there lived the Reays
Who did their bit in many ways
John Dickinson was Catchem John
His hasty manner smiled upon.

Coffee Johnny was a local tramp
Who slept out in the cold and damp.
Under hedges of nearby farms
Only inside when in barns.

Bainbridge Buildings, one fine morn
Was where Joe Allison was born,
A miner best part of his life
He has experienced joy and strife.

Piggy Turner lived nearby.
So called-you'll know the reason why
If you recall that awful smell
The pigs were feeding, you could tell.

One market garden was Dicky Rowe's
How he lived so long nobody knows
It could be never ending toil
Trending plants and digging soil.

Harris had gardens too.
For tomatoes one had to queue.
They has greenhouses and lots of land
On which their fine house did stand.

Hall, Jameson and Somerville
Some of their work stands strongly still
Shoes were mended, bricks were laid
Each an expert at his trade.

Mr Nairn, fine suits he's sewn.
Which any man was proud to own
A Tailor, deft with thread and pin
He also played the violin.

Lilly Duffell delivered mail
In all weathers – rain and hail
She still lives on North Avenue
And no doubt could tell a tail or two.

Mr Kendal riding passed
On his bike – more slow than fast
He hope the folks weren't very? Ill
And would get some time with a pill.

Mr Reed taught at the school
He was well liked and there to rule
He rode a bike and smoked a pipe
At the same time – "The old school Type".

To those who did their very best
To make this place "Hope of the West"
The tribute to them all must be
That this goes down in history.